RENO

RISING

Compiled by Susan Ackerman: www.renorising.com

Project managed by Follow It Thru Publishing: heatherandrews.press

ISBN: 978-1-5136-3627-6

Acknowledgments

I truly believe that no one ever creates success alone.

Thank you to my thirteen co-authors for your willingness to go deep and share such personal and private moments of your life with us. You have shared your stories, your hearts, your pain, and your triumphs with me, and I am honored that you trusted me enough to join in this project. I have learned so much from each of you, and I respect and admire you all so much. Thank you for sharing in my vision and for joining me on this journey. I am so honored to share this book with each of you.

Thank you to Heather Andrews and her team at Follow it Thru Publishing. Thank you for your patience, your willingness to think outside the box, and for nurturing my idea into an amazing creation. I could not have done this without you.

Thank you to Taylor Boone for sharing in my vision and sharing your incredible talent with us. It's crazy how a chance meeting can turn your life upside down. I'm so glad you followed the nudge to join me on this project.

Thank you to Emily Golden for offering her time, talent, and resources to create an amazingly powerful video to accompany Reno Rising. Your vision and passion for women continue to inspire me. I am so thankful to have met you, and I am blessed to call you my friend.

Contents

Foreword

Our city continues to be on the rise, and women are leading the way. Reno faces challenges caused by the adversity in the past, but as mayor, I'm more hopeful than ever before. It starts by recognizing where we've been and where we're going.

Today, women have more opportunities than ever, with limitless potential right at our fingertips.

Our sisterhood can be such a powerful force, but we must be united and supportive of each other. I've spent far too many hours perplexed by the new communication age of social media where negative and cruel comments have become the norm—especially towards the important women in our lives. I want us all to take our power back by remembering to post with purpose and kindness.

Sadly, our culture has pushed us to shrink from recognition, validation, and lifting each other up.

It's time we supported one another. The women you'll hear from in these chapters are doing exactly that.

We have visionaries from every generation included in this book. But there are thousands more who could read these pages and shape our region's future. I'm excited to see those successes and fresh ideas blossom here along the Truckee River.

That's why I feel honored to recognize these fourteen strong and passionate women who have worked tirelessly to make a difference in our city. They have truly helped Reno to rise.

Hillary L. Schieve,
Mayor,
City of Reno.

Introduction

The Dream

Sometimes, when you least expect it, something incredible happens to change your life, your purpose, and your world. On October 16, 2017, a simple Facebook post started with, *Are you looking for an amazing office space for your creative business…* and the rest, as they say, is history.

I wasn't honestly in the market for a new office space. For the past ten years, I was a work-from-home entrepreneur. First, as a leader in a direct sales company, and eventually adding on the role of women's empowerment coach. But something was missing. I was restless. No longer challenged in my direct sales business (or so I told myself) and questioning my direction in coaching, I was desperate for a change. The truth was, I had fallen into a deep depression. My days were spent going from television show to television show with a nap strategically placed somewhere in between. I hated leaving my house. Even a quick trip to the grocery store was a chore. I rarely got dressed in the morning and even taking the time to shower and put on makeup seemed pointless. I had lost any sense of purpose and direction for my life and didn't really care about myself or anything else for that matter.

And then, there it was. This innocuous post on my newsfeed shared from a friend of a friend looking for an office mate. I wasn't sure if I even had a business at this point that could pay rent, but I was intrigued and interested just the same. I decided it couldn't hurt to look, so I replied and set up a time to see the available space.

The building was beautiful. An old mansion right on the Truckee River, in an area of Reno I had never visited before. Nicole met me outside, hugged me like we were old friends, and led me in the front door. The space she wanted was lovely. There were three rooms. The first, a beautiful nook with a window seat, surrounded by windows and overlooking the river was warm and inviting. There was a larger room attached and then a project room – full of cabinets, and ample workspace. I could see why she, as an interior designer, fell in love with it. For me, however, I wasn't sure.

I wandered across the hall into what reminded me of a large old parlor—complete with a beautiful old fireplace. Judges panels, crown molding, and deep rich paint colors added to the beauty of the space. The multiple windows filled the room with sunshine and warmth. It reminded me of the old Victorian homes I had always loved in the magazines. Visions filled my mind, and I could immediately see round tables, and women, and a speaker at the fireplace. There was laughter, collaboration, and a sense of community. I wandered through the room into the attached butler's pantry, feeling an energy I had never felt before. I could see coffee cups on the shelves—each with a message—and teacups. Beautiful tea cups and teapots and flavorful teas. On the other side of the butler's pantry was an office …My office. I don't know how I knew, I just knew. I could feel it. I placed my hands on the wall, and the energy surged through me. I was home. This was where I belonged.

I spoke with the owner of the property and inquired about leasing this other space, and she told me it was not available. She explained that she was in negotiation with an attorney's office who wanted the entire building—minus the suite my new friend Nicole was interested in. She was only interested in leasing the entire building. It was more than I could take on, so disappointed, I made my way home.

For the next two weeks, I thought of nothing but this building, the space, and my new office. I couldn't sleep. How could I take on the entire building? It seemed so much bigger than me and yet, I had a sureness, a knowing that this space was going to be a women's entrepreneurial development center; a space for women to come and find support, encouragement, and community. A place where women would be able to step into their own greatness and a place where women could be inspired. I contacted the owner and told her my idea. That was November 1. On January 1, 2018, Inspire Reno opened to the public.

A New Purpose

My vision had become a reality. The round tables filled the parlor—women were attending workshops and events. There was laughter, community, and collaboration. My pantry was stocked with over seventy-five coffee mugs—each with an inspirational and uplifting message—and beautifully decorated teacups welcoming the women that poured into them. Other female entrepreneurs filled the office spaces on the second floor, and Nicole (the woman who placed the original ad) moved into the space of her dreams across the hall. It was a dream come true, a new purpose, a reason to wake up in the morning. Every day was a new adventure, and as I watched more and more women walk through the door. I was filled with more passion for my dream than ever before.

The women I had the pleasure to meet filled my soul. Their stories inspired and encouraged me. So many women fighting the system, fighting to make their place in the world, fighting for their dreams. All of them desperately wanting a community to feel secure in, a community free of drama, free of competition, free of pain. A community of women that encouraged them, celebrated them, and believed in them.

The Inspiration

I wish I could tell you the inspiration for this project came from uplifting stories shared by other women, but the opposite is true. The real story behind this project are the painful stories that were shared in confidence with me. Stories of women in corporate America who were judged by their looks, their size, and the color of their lipstick. Stories of women wanting to be free from gossip, competition, judgment, and jealousy that followed them in the workplace. Others who had dreams and aspirations but were told not to bother trying—that they would never succeed, that they were doomed for failure. And then myself running into a person who, after a disagreement, publicly berated and belittled me for my age, weight, and thinning hair by publicly posting on social media, *how can this woman who is fifty-three—fat and balding—call herself a life coach?*

So many stories, and so many women. I was so sad for them, for me, and for all women who had to live with this. I couldn't understand how we, as women, could have come so far and yet still have so much further to go. I was angry at the "bullies," both men and women who felt it was okay to be mean, okay to cast judgment, okay to berate other human beings to make themselves feel better or more powerful, or whatever it is they felt because of their actions. I longed for the Pollyanna world where women would work together, and people lived happily ever after.

I wondered how I could take on the oppressors, make a change, create a call to action where women said NO MORE and where women could band together to lift each other, support each other, and celebrate each other. A place where women could step into their own power—not to tear someone else down—not to point fingers in blame—but instead to lift each other up. A place where positive action could create a huge difference.

A Movement

The vision of *Reno Rising* began to grow in my heart. The more stories I heard, the stronger my desire grew. This was an opportunity for women in Reno to reach out and lift other women in Reno. An invitation to our sisters to link arm in arm with us; to rise to their purpose, in their greatness, and into who they were created to be. Reno women who have experienced pain and loss — reaching out to others experiencing the same things. Women who have been repressed (sometimes by themselves), refusing to remain a victim of their circumstance reaching out to others who are still trapped within theirs. A book created by women for women. Stories of hope, stories of courage, stories of victory. A book for every woman, written by every woman.

My hope, as you read the following chapters, is that you find yourself somewhere within the pages of these stories and that you would allow these women — in your own community — to bring you courage. The experiences are real. The feelings and emotions shared so freely are also real. Every woman who took part in this project wants you to know that you are not alone. Whatever you are facing, whatever circumstances are holding you back, and whatever fears you might have do not need to define who you are and what you do with your future. Each of us invites you to "rise up" to the person you were created to be and to join us in this positive movement where women lift other women. And know, if you are reading this right now and don't feel strong enough, that we are here to lift you until you are strong enough to lift yourself!

My original vision for this project has taken on a life of its own. As the excitement of our creation grew, *Reno Rising* started to become so much more than just a book. It has become a movement. Reno Rising is volume one in the *Rising Across America* series. Other cities are waiting to create their own volumes and join the cause. I am so proud of the women who stepped forward to share their stories with you, and I pray that you are inspired by their willingness to share such intensely private moments of their life. There were many tears shed in the writing of these chapters. It is frightening to be so open and vulnerable with others. I applaud their bravery and their willingness to put their fears aside, and I am honored to have grown with each of these women on their journey.

I hope that you too will join us in our journey! You, my friend, have been created for a very specific purpose. Your life has meaning. You are powerful. You have been created for greatness. It is your time. It is our time. Stand with us my friend and let us together change the world.

Susan Ackerman,
Director,
Reno Rising.

My Shining Star

By Julia Picetti

What does it mean to rise up?

I assume the definition is different for everyone. However, there seems to be a common thread in all who decide to rise up even through the most adverse circumstances.

Not just once, but, over and over again, we get knocked down. Yet, we continue to rise.

That common thread seems to be explained with words of character that have been my rock for as long as I can remember. When I meet others who instill this essence, I can feel it.

I can *feel* faith, persistence, a positive attitude, grit, stubbornness, strength, courage and most of all, love for myself and others.

My journey has not been easy. In fact, it has been really difficult.

I was an only child growing up, and even though my parents loved me, I was certainly not their priority. I was neglected; I was abused, physically, verbally, and sexually. By the time I was fifteen, I had had enough of my home life situation and moved out on my own, which left me homeless for a better part of two years.

Somehow, I felt okay about this…even at the tender age of fifteen. Call it youth, call it stupidity, or maybe just call it a peaceful knowing in the middle of my storm. I knew that I would be okay.

I am a fighter; not only for myself, but also for others. It's with that burning desire to rise up that I become the best I can be without any doubt. But with all that I went through in my earlier years, there was *nothing* (or so I thought) that could prepare me for the most tragic event one could ever experience:

9

Losing a child.

I had Jane Aubrey, my first born, at the age of twenty. In a lot of ways, she saved my life. She gave me a *real* purpose to grow and thrive.

I wanted to be the best mom that she could have, full of love and understanding with everything that I wasn't afforded as a child.

Jane was a very bright girl. In fact, I often referred to her as my shining star. Jane was in the gifted and talented program. She danced for over ten years and was also involved with the theater. She had a voice that was of an angel, I used to have her sing for me all the time. Before she became ill, Jane was my best friend. We always laughed together, danced together, and shopped together. In fact, San Francisco was our favorite place to go shopping several times a year. She had a blessed, happy childhood. I have many photos capturing our precious time together. Everyone loved her energy, and when she walked into a room, you knew it. She was always such a joy to be with.

I also have two other children. Gage, Jane's younger brother, is always filled with joy and constantly has a huge smile on his face. Then there's Anna, the baby of the family who has taught us all what it is like to love deeply and has been the glue to our family.

Through most of their childhood I was a single mom with my head down, working and creating a good life for us all. I educated myself through books; I love reading, especially anything inspirational. And, of course, I had my strong faith in God.

Life certainly wasn't perfect, but it was good. We had a lot of love in our small family. I finally met my husband when the children were all young; Jane was fourteen. We got married and quickly became a blended family with a total of five children.

When I sit quietly and think back about my daughter, I realize that I started losing her when she was very young.

I noticed Jane was starting to go through what I thought to be simply teenage attitude, what some call 'the angst years'. It was so bad that I had us both in therapy (separate and then together). It was very difficult, but after three to four years of steadily attending sessions, it started to level out. We could finally feel some relief.

I always thought to myself, *this isn't who I raised.*

Being a good mom was the most important, precious thing I could ever do. I had no understanding of her behavior, and sadly, I didn't receive any answers from the professionals I reached out to for help. Little did I know that Jane was on her way to having a mental illness called borderline personality disorder (BPD).

She was finally diagnosed when she was eighteen. Unfortunately, there are no medications to help BPD. You can have intense talk therapy, but there is no cure for BPD. It is one of the worst mental illnesses that one can be diagnosed with. Those that suffer from BPD have many disorders under the BPD umbrella such as eating disorders, cutting, risky behavior, anger, substance abuse disorder, major depressive disorder, confusion and the deepest sadness that one can ever have. Jane had them all, and it was heartbreaking to see her in the grips of this awful illness.

Unfortunately, many people choose to self-medicate in order to find some relief from the symptoms. Sadly, for us, that was the case with my Jane. It wasn't until she was twenty-one that I realized that she was smoking meth, heroin, and any other substance she could get her hands on just to make her feel something other than despair.

I fought for her for her life and for her sanity.

On March 9, 2015, I got a call from my auntie, who lives about ten minutes away from my house in Reno. Jane had been living with her for a while, and she seemed to be doing well. She had gone back to school, and she was looking forward to starting a new job where she would be making more money than she ever had. We were all so hopeful *and* proud of her.

However, Jane wasn't going to start her job or finish her schooling. She overdosed on meth and heroin alone in her room.

When I got that call, I was sitting at the computer doing some work at home. I remember it was an overcast day, but it was nice out. Anna had just gotten home from school, and all were getting settled into their afternoon routine. When I spoke to my aunt over the phone, prompting me to go to her house immediately, I could hear the deep sorrow in her voice. It was nothing like I had heard before.

I had no idea what was to come. I had no idea my daughter was dead.

All I could do was simply say okay and hang up the phone.

As I pulled up to my aunt's house, there were firetrucks, police, and an ambulance. I frantically ran in and was told that Jane was no longer with us. I screamed and ran to her room in shear panic. I instinctively crawled on top of her, screaming and begging her to wake up.

"*We got this baby,*" I repeated over and over to her.

"*We got this.*"

Jane, my shining star, had lost her light. She was almost twenty-five.

The pain that ripped through me was—and still is—something that I can't really explain.

There really are no words for such devastation.

Suddenly, and for days after it happened, I couldn't really hear anything. It was like I had cotton stuffed in my head; my balance was off, and my entire body ached so badly that I could hardly walk or have the strength to open a door. I didn't eat for days and days, and I drank a lot.

This lasted for months.

Thankfully, the one constant that I had, that even Jane's death could not take away, was my faith in Jesus. Deep down inside I knew he was there, beside me in my pain.

When Jane died, I soon realized that God *had* in fact been preparing me for this moment for my entire life. Every painful experience that I had endured in my life up until Jane's death was an experience that I needed to have so when the real tragedy happened, I would be able to have the strength to crawl out of the darkness and rise again.

To rise for Him, for me, for my kids, and for others.

I am very involved in my church. I volunteer often and have grown close to the staff. Many of the members are my dear friends. Because of these friendships, my faith, and my community who wrapped their loving arms around me, I was able to finally start coming out of my deep darkness.

I will always remember the day that I woke up and came out into my kitchen. I stood at my sink quietly and looked out my window into my beautiful backyard. For the first time since Jane died, I could hear the birds singing, and I could see the sun shining.

My husband had made coffee and was cooking bacon next to me. Finally, I could smell, actually *smell*, the bacon. It was at that moment that I felt a tiny burst of joy, so small, that if I had not been present in that moment, I would have missed it.

I know it was God's way of letting me know that I was going to be okay. Then, just as quickly as the feeling came, it was gone. But it certainly was *not* forgotten. I clung to that moment with everything I had, knowing that I had to *rise up* in order to save myself.

One of the many emotions you go through when you are grieving is anger.

I started to become angry thinking about how I had fought so hard for Jane—for her sanity, her addiction, and her recovery. I also fought for the professionals to help her in a dignified, responsible way. I realized, through the struggle I had with all of it, that others were going through the same hell.

About five months after Jane's death, my church, Grace Church, approached me and said that they wanted to get more involved in helping provide solutions to addiction and mental health in our community. I, of course, said yes, and suggested that we start the conversation in our congregation about addiction and mental health.

Each week there are many people sitting and listening to the word of God who are struggling. Many are filled with shame; the shame of having an addiction or a family member who may be suffering. Each year, Grace Church collects an offering called a Year-End Gift. The church takes these gifts and donates them to organizations within our community to help where there is a need.

One thing led to another, and the Year-End Gift that year was the largest that Grace Church has ever raised.

The money was used to purchase a home for young women who struggle with opiate addiction. It is a home that offers long-term recovery with mental health solutions and back to work programs, all in a loving home environment. It is called The Jane Aubrey House.

I worked my body tirelessly to get this home remodeled for these young ladies. It was a team effort full of love from people who attend Grace Church and the leaders in our community. Every wall that was torn down and rebuilt, the kitchen was completely redone, and new flooring was installed throughout. Each stroke of the paintbrush, every tree that was removed, and all the weeds that were pulled and replaced with beautiful flowers were all steps I took through my healing.

It wasn't just healing for myself; I was also healing for all those that continue to struggle and fight for themselves and their loved ones every single day.

I have become an instrumental piece to Grace Church's three-year campaign in an effort to secure six-million dollars to build other houses like The Jane Aubrey House. This campaign will take half of the money and put it towards the community of Reno to build additional homes to serve those that are affiliated with addiction.

These homes provide a long-term, family environment with wrap-around services that include mental health. So far, we have four homes total and have saved hundreds of lives.

It has been over three years since my Janie has died. In fact, as I write this, it is just a few days from her birthday, June 4, 1989. She would have been twenty-nine this coming day.

I can feel my mind swirling.

My anxiety is up. I'm not sleeping. I have nightmares, and my memory isn't as it should be. My body is starting to hurt, and I feel like I'm sinking into deep sorrow. I never really know how long this wave of grief will last. It can be anywhere from a couple of days to several weeks, stuck in this dread of not having my beautiful daughter to laugh with or dance with, and knowing that I will never hear her beautiful voice again.

Thankfully (and not so thankfully), I usually only get this twice a year—on her birthday because she is not here, and on the date of her death. I suppose it will be like this for the rest of my life. A pain that I will have to endure.

I had a woman once look at me and say, "Julia, I am so sorry you have had such a hard life."

When I heard this, I looked at her with kindness in my eyes and said, "I don't see it that way. In fact, it has allowed me to be there for others with real understanding and love."

I have been in the therapist's chair since I was nineteen, hashing out all the hurtful moments in my life, all that I have had to experience, witness, and feel. I was told by one of my first therapists that I reminded her of a beautiful flower. This flower *had* bloomed in the desert, in harsh conditions, with very little water. I didn't understand that statement for many, many years.

Several therapists and even more years later, I not only understand that statement, but have come to embrace it.

When I look back on my life and all that I have had the blessing to learn, through so much pain and struggle, I know that God has given me everything that I needed to not only rise, but to rise for Him, for me, and most of all for others.

Julia Picetti

Julia Picetti was born in Reno, Nevada. In her free time, she loves to read books, go hiking, spend time with her family and friends and enjoy all that is offered in her community. She has sold real estate since 1995 and is very involved in her church and community.

Julia has worked tirelessly as a project manager for two non-profits in the recovery sector to help those who struggle with addiction. She has also been a speaker at a TEDx event about the opioid epidemic that has stricken our country and the fight she endured for her daughter.

Just like Jane, who always had a heart for those that had less, Julia will continue her outreach for those who suffer from addiction, mental illness, and homelessness.

Bought for A Price

By Sonya Lan

"I've never met a strong person with an easy past."
~Unknown

My story is a long time in the making. Originally, I planned on writing a cutesy how-to chapter about running a profitable business as a woman and leaving my life story out of it.

I'm currently in a good place. I am a business coach and the founder of Pearls, a non-profit organization providing faith-based outreach and support for women in the sex industry, including victims and survivors of the commercialized sexual exploitation and trafficking. Still, I wasn't always an entrepreneur or activist. I would love to tell a flowery story of how I made it to that point, but there are some parts I spent a huge chunk of my life doing drugs to forget. I know how easy it is to lose sight of the love in your life when trying to claw your way out of a fiery pit. I know how tempting it is to drown your memories, your sorrows. You may feel empty inside, trying to fill that hollow space with something other than shame. In fact, my past was a source of shame until I wrote this book. It was most obvious when other women would try to exchange stories. Whenever my time came to share, I wanted desperately to skip my turn. It would be one thing if I had just smoked weed every day for a year and emotionally checked out. Instead, my life was a series of terrible situations and bad decisions beyond the average person's daily battles. Still, I would do a disservice to the women I serve by hiding that.

Truthfully, pretending everything is okay just makes it harder, makes you feel more alone. Sociologically speaking, women use these stories as a currency of sorts, investing in feelings of friendship and cultivating trust over time. How could I short-change my fellow woman? Instead, I offer a gritty, honest, and pure love letter to the many women who have been through absolute hell or are still in it. This is the microphone for the voiceless, women fighting an invisible struggle alongside 'regular' folk. If you were looking for a sign or a big push, here it is. I'm going to share my story and my transformation so you can see the possibilities lying just beneath all the suffering. This also serves as a reminder to all of us that God can, and will, use anyone.

Family of Origin

My life was tumultuous from the beginning. My mom and dad divorced when I was two years old. My older sister and I lived with my father and grandmother, but the church was our second home. My dad was a deacon at a Korean Baptist church and we were there all day on Wednesday's, Friday's, and Sunday's. The church's message was extremely conservative, always about fire and brimstone. They loved teaching us about Noah and the Ark, emphasizing the fact that God drowned the world because of their sin.

They neglected to share the love of God or all the wondrous miracles Jesus performed while here on Earth. All I thought about was punishment and ways to avoid it, even at an early age. At age eleven, I had a spiritual encounter with the Lord at a church camp. I felt so much love, and after that, I had a hunger to worship him. I would even see images of the Lord in the sky. I could feel His love as it enveloped me, and I've carried that moment in my heart ever since. This forever changed my view of God and religion.

School would prove to be my best form of escape. Before, I would be sitting at the table with my grandmother, practicing my ABC's on the back of Korean calendars while she called me "babo," which means stupid in Korean. She didn't have an education or great quality of life, which she seemed to take out on me. My dad remarried a few years later, and we moved in with my step-mom. It was extremely emotionally abusive and, at times, physically abusive. For example, when I used to wash dishes at the age of five, my step-mom would degrade me because there were still spots on some of the dishes, and even hit me with a pan once. Things continued this way for years.

Looking back, I see now that it was normal in Korean culture for parents to put their children down and pressure them to do better. That pressure never really leaves kids as they grow into adults, and sometimes manifests itself in horrible ways. I took on that baggage until I turned twelve, when I finally ran away to my mother's house. You might wonder what would tip me over the edge after all the abuse I was used to. My step-mom had thrown rotten milk on me before I had left for school. I told my best friend, then my mom, who said to tell my dad. My father didn't believe what I told him, and I was punished. He placed the blame on me because my step-mom lied. My mother told me and my sister to pack, but to still act like we were going to school. We put our clothes in plastic bags, and my mom picked us up across the street from school. Later that week, my mom went over to my dad's house with a gallon of milk to throw on my step-mom. I can still picture the look on her face as milk dripped down it.

My dad and step-mom divorced shortly after we moved to my mom's. My dad got kicked out of the church because of his divorce. You would think that we'd be in a better environment with my mom, but she was in an extremely abusive relationship. I'm talking knife-fight abusive. By this point, she'd completely lost her mind. She let us do whatever we wanted. She let us stay at friends' houses overnight, and when we returned, she would throw anything she could find at us. My mom was so caught up in my stepdad's cheating that she didn't pay attention to any of us. She paid more attention to alcohol in hopes that it would get through the pain. She would call us nigger children. This was her way to reject us since we wanted to move back in with my dad, who was Korean and black. We also had a younger sister who stayed with my mother.

My older sister started having sex and doing drugs, as did my younger sisters. I lost my virginity at the age of twelve. Of course, the guy dumped me. I was already used to being rejected, though, so that became the norm for me. Over time, my mom realized she'd bitten off more than she could chew by taking me and my sister into her home. We called my dad and moved back with him. At this point, I chose to sacrifice love and warmth for stability. Still, I ended up moving back with my mom because I stole from a department store and I didn't want him to know. I was afraid of the punishment. Ultimately, my parents went to court for custody, and my mother won. My siblings and I had to testify against my father and say that he abused us. My life after that went by very fast. My siblings and I were out of control, and so was my mother. We were having sex, doing drugs, stealing cars, and more.

We eventually moved to Stockton. I met two girls, and they introduced me to their friends, who were gang members. Later I got jumped as an initiation into the gang. We called ourselves L.O.C. aka, Loced Out Cuties. I met and dated a man named Tony, who was nineteen. I was thirteen, almost fourteen, but I told him I was sixteen. He had taken me and my friends home one night, and my friends told me I should hook-up with him for a ride. That's exactly what I did, and it escalated into a full-blown relationship. I started doing crank at the same time.

The first time, I went to a friend of my friend's house, which happened to belong to a thirty-five-year-old man. I didn't want to sniff the crank, so they put it in a piece of toilet paper, and I drank it with water to get high. Soon after, I started doing acid, drinking, and running away from cops. I got caught one day, and the cops brought me home to my mother. They told her I was at the house of an ex-felon, but the reality of getting caught meant nothing to me.

After the police left, I called my friends and asked them to pick me up down the street from my house. I told my mom I was going outside to swim and went to the backyard and slipped out the back gate. Eventually, I wouldn't have to sneak around; my mother was doing drugs, and I would go with her to get her drugs. She would trip out and think people were breaking into the house and cause complete chaos.

I experienced another heartbreak with Tony; he cheated on me. The entire situation was crazy, which led me and my friends to try to beat the girl up. I was never able to get to her, but it ended with me letting Tony know he gave me chlamydia. I shared my antibiotics with him, and we continued our relationship, much to the dismay of my friends. He stopped messing around with the other girl. I spent more time with him and less time with my friends. I stopped doing drugs, drinking, and getting into trouble. Did I say drugs? Well, to me alcohol and cigarettes didn't count. My mother allowed Tony to move with us back to the Tacoma/Seattle area when I was fourteen. I ended up pregnant shortly after, and my mother wanted me to get an abortion. That wasn't something I wanted, so she became physically abusive and kicked me in the stomach. The only thing that saved me was my aunt who called the police and had my mother arrested. After some hesitation, my other aunt and uncle supported our decision to keep our child.

The first time I saw any emotion other than anger from my dad is when he found out I was having a child. He cried. He also told me not to have an abortion and that he would support me so that I could finish school. I was shocked. My father later refused to help me, avoided me, and didn't answer any of my calls. It was as if I wasn't his daughter anymore. During this time, my mom even accused me of sleeping with my stepfather, and I found out my grandmother was doing crack. I moved to California when my baby, Tony, was about three weeks old. I lived with my boyfriend and his family, but I realized I wanted more for myself. I left my boyfriend and moved back home with my mom. Big Tony (my son's father) kept begging me to come back, but I didn't return.

I found out my older sister was a stripper by seeing her onstage. My friend and I had gone into the club to get her a job. Right before I turned eighteen, I was encouraged by my girlfriend's mother to try working as an escort. For my first call, I thought it was a just going to be a dinner date; I was shocked to find out that I was supposed to sleep with him. He was around sixty years old. At this point I just figured, I'm already doing it for free and being used by guys, so why not? I did my 'job' in the most literal sense. My younger sister also got into the industry by using my ID to work at the legal brothels in Reno. I didn't know about this until she returned home one day from her graduation trip to Mexico with $10,000. Going to work in Nevada to work at the brothels terrified me, and rightfully so. They were catty and vicious, and the women were downright mean. For example, one woman filled another woman's shampoo bottle with Nair hair removal cream because she would "dirty hustle." If one of the women was talking to a guy at the bar, this particular girl would cut right in and steal the customer. We were in an environment where we were in competition with each other, so we had to do everything to protect ourselves and our income. At this particular 'ranch' (brothel) the owners and management had favorites, and of course, the top booker, so the top bookers would get special treatment. This particular owner would sleep with the working girls. I saw the manipulation and the hold that the owner had over these ladies, so once the owner began making advances towards me, I left.

The owners at the new ranch I worked at got me a place, furniture, and even an attorney for custody. My mom came to visit, and soon I found myself giving her money to gamble. I convinced her to work with me at the ranch since she didn't have a boyfriend anymore and all her kids were grown. She was hired, but began to take my customers and badmouth me to them. She became my competition by dirty hustling. We had a meeting with one of the owners, and these issues were resolved by moving us into separate working rooms. My mother had also moved out of my home and into her own place off the golf course.

While at that ranch, I continued to do cocaine and started doing crystal meth with two of the girls there. Normally, I would never do drugs at work, but you are who you hang out with. I would skip lineup when I would hear the buzzard.

I met a man and almost ended up getting pimped out by a client, although I didn't know he was a pimp at the time. I traveled to see him and dated him while I was still trying to date Chad, an abusive alcoholic who would become my husband (and ex-husband). I even did porn in Florida during this time. Then I found out I was pregnant with my second child. That didn't stop me from doing cocaine or drinking because I planned to get an abortion. When I was five months, I had a huge scare from doing too many drugs and drinking too much alcohol. After that, I decided I wanted to keep my baby. I left the business and married Chad.

While living the married life, I had a business in the beauty industry. I left Chad because of the abuse and then forgave him. This went on for a long time until I couldn't take it anymore and went back to work at the brothel. I knew the only way that the only way to be rid of him was to leave the state, so I moved across the country and started over in Reno, Nevada.

In 2007, I was leaving work after drinking to pick up some cocaine and meth when I got into an accident. I was arrested and lost custody of my kids. I quit working and moved back to Washington with my family. I did crack for the first time with my hairdresser and my mother. I wanted to numb myself. The pain was too much to bear alone and sober. From there, I returned to the industry. I made a lot of money, almost got pimped out again, was hurt so bad by a customer that I needed stitches, went back to jail, and more.

I met a man named Dan, and we dated off and on for a year. He found out about what I did for a profession, so I quit the industry again and walked into Summit Church for a women's bible study.

The Healing

That's when I started my healing journey. I noticed that God had been trying to reach me through my brokenness and lonely nights, and I could feel him pulling me back to Him. It was a long ride filled with twist and turns, just like the rest of my life. I got pregnant with Liana and married Dan. Marriage and pregnancy were extremely difficult. I was at a low. I had thought about suicide. I was emotional during my restoration; my past rejection kept getting triggered every time Dan would reject and leave me. There were times I wanted to give up on myself and marriage. The industry was tempting because that life was comfortable, familiar.

When our second daughter was born, we were on the verge of divorce, but we separated instead. I was acting out of my pain from being rejected, which led to anger and violence. He was acting out of pain from his past, which caused him to emotionally shut down. We were working against each other.

He and I eventually got some help. I was also led to write my book. While doing research, I found the Treasures Ministry. It's a ministry that reaches out to women in the sex industry. I couldn't believe there were other women out there like me! I was ecstatic. I had finally found my 'tribe' of sorts. I went to a training to start an outreach in my area and quickly realized I needed more healing. I attended a support group at Treasures and went back to Breaking Free (Restoration Ministry) for the third time to specifically deal with the shame of my prostitution. I was introduced to the prophetic, and I felt the love of Jesus. I was reminded of the time I encountered Him at church camp. I moved back to Reno, met The Soars, and experienced more breakthrough and healing from speaking and attending sessions at the Tahoe Mission School. My restoration and freedom continued after this.

Throughout the last nine years of my life, I have grown closer to Jesus and know who He is, who I am. Although my marriage and family are not restored, I am. I learned how to be a loving mother to my children and a loving daughter to the one who created me.

During this journey, I have founded Pearls, which is a non-profit 501c3 organization helping women in the sex industry in Southern California and Reno, Nevada. I have my bachelor's degree. I am a certified life and business coach, and I'm in the process of adding education, business training, and housing to my organization. I am also the co-founder of a soon to be launched tech company that will enable peer-to-peer RV/boat share. I am at the peak of my life. I'm not saying that to brag, but to give you hope for your future! Like I said, I don't look like what I've been through, and I'm forever grateful for that. My life is a living testament to the love and restorative power of God.

Do you see the pattern in my life, in yours? Do you see an endpoint involving acceptance and love? Were you raised by someone who, instead of being warm or kind, was strict or emotionally unavailable? Growing up, all I wanted was to feel love and affection from my dad. For all his faults, he was always busy providing the basics and raising us. He showed love through providing for us financially. This made me look at my mom and why their marriage didn't work. She was very much in tune with her emotions, despite trauma and abuse from her childhood that was worse than mine. When you are with a man who is emotionally unavailable, it solidifies the rejection and trauma in your life, so you feel that you are unworthy of love. This can be passed down to you, or you can end the cycle and make new rules for your life. It's hard and tedious at times and needs to be built on a foundation of understanding. For me, God was that foundation. Nothing else was quite strong enough. The understanding and compassion I now have for my mother is due to my own experiences. I realized I had just recreated this cycle of hers in my intimate relationships. All I ever dreamed of was to be a mama and wife. Yet, my brokenness led me to settle for the first man to show me affection. I jumped into relationships too fast, became super 'needy' and ended up being abused, either emotionally and/or physically, time after time! I was oblivious to how broken I was and the healing that I needed, so I continued to make bad choices. Healing is so crucial to moving forward in life and having healthy, loving relationships. Unfortunately, I chose men who were like my father.

Somehow, there was a sense of comfort and stability that I felt, so I discounted my needs and basic right to be treated like a human being. I made excuses for men who treated me poorly. I continued to think it was me while they got the pass to continue the way they were: abusive. I saw the same cycle in my family lineage. It was up to me to break that curse in my family.

As I write this chapter, I have no hate or anger towards my mom and dad. I'm not trying to expose them; I am merely bringing things to light so others who need healing from trauma in childhood can come out of that dark place and take small steps toward healing. It's about acknowledging that you haven't been treated well; for some, this may be hard when dealing with Stockholm Syndrome, an unhealthy connection between excusing their behavior and lessening our abuse. I could see that the people who caused trauma in my life had pasts filled with abandonment, brokenness, abuse, and struggles that were way worse than mine. Keep in mind; I'm not discounting my abuse and trauma. Rather, I'm looking back on that feeling through the lens of healing. I was able to see the hurt and pain they received from their parents, but refused to acknowledge their inability to choose to heal. I was overwhelmed with compassion for them.

Then I looked even further and saw the life both my grandmothers had to live in Korea, the abuse and abandonment they too had to endure. I gained more compassion for my family, and motivation to break that cycle. You can only come to a place of peace after you take the necessary steps to heal and be healed; otherwise, you are just excusing their abuse toward you. As you have read this chapter, I hope you have processed it from a place of empowerment, with faith that your empowerment will turn into compassion and healing. Know that there is nothing that you can't recover from. Are you ready to take your life back? Are you ready to experience the love and fulfillment you deserve? Then you're in the right place, reading the right chapter at the right time. Your time is now, and you were born for such a time as this!

Sonya Lan

Sonya Lan is a proud mama to seven children and her fur baby, Peanut Girl. She is passionate about raising her children and reaching the world with spiritual truths in love (Jesus).

Sonya has been a serial entrepreneur. She is CEO of Sonya Lan LLC, a corporation that teaches entrepreneurs to create, market and launch successfully into their God-given destiny. She also is founder and CEO of Unleashed Global Network/Pearls, a non-profit charity that reaches women in the adult entertainment industry with the message that they are loved and valued.

Sonya is creator of Design Your Destiny, Unleash Your Vision Online Business Course and 90 Day Planner. Her purpose is to help other passion driven women unleash into their destiny. Her life's message is all about love, healing and building the kingdom.

For fun Sonya loves skiing, reading a good book, and the beach.

Chickens Can Dream Big Too

By Laura Watson

The riddle, "why'd the chicken cross the road?" never really made sense to me, until the day I realized I *was* the chicken, unsure of how to cross. I enviously watched others as they successfully crossed their own roads, wishing I had the guts to follow suit and pursue some big dream.

I've actually had the perfect life for a chicken. It's been average, risk-free, and I've never had any reason to complain, except for the fact that I spent so much of my life fearing disapproval and ridicule. I have always been painfully shy. From a young age, my red hair and freckles always made me stand out in a crowd. Every well-intentioned compliment made my pale skin turn bright red; every joke saw my face burn crimson. My skeletal figure added to the very unwelcome comments through middle school and high school. In middle school, my best friend, who was like a sister to me since I was three years old, dumped me for her popular and pretty friends. Shy, awkward, grossly underweight, and fearing further rejection, I started to hate my life. Struggling with depression and feeling like I never fit in, I hated going to school. It was difficult developing close friendships because I was too terrified to speak. When I went on social outings with the few friends I did have, I desperately wanted to get my nerve up to talk to people, but more often than not, I required a little (or a lot) of liquid courage. I was a quiet, meek, personality-less nobody, trying to hide how I felt about myself. I have spent my entire life playing it safe and trying to seek approval from others.

Of course, my life had its highlights. I loved my first high school job working at a daycare center, which saw me obtain my Bachelor's in Child Development to become a teacher. As a teacher, I felt like I was doing something that mattered, and I never felt shy or judged around my adoring students. Committed to my career, I worked to obtain my Master's in Education. During these years, I married a wonderful guy that always made me laugh, and we had two healthy, beautiful girls. When the girls reached school age, I reluctantly quit my career to focus on being a mom. Without my additional income, we decided to leave Orange County and moved to Reno. As the girls continued their schooling, I volunteered so I could still work with kids, and I became friends with some of the other moms. My husband worked from home for a software company and gathered investment properties on the side. Nothing exciting. Just doing the things I was supposed to be doing. I had gone thirty-seven years with seemingly nothing to write about. My life was what I had made it, and everything I had ever asked for.

Aside from the highlight reel, I continued to hate how shy and quiet I was, and how awkward I always felt. I felt like my life was lacking something, or that I was meant to be doing something different. I was the chicken that desperately wanted to cross the road but couldn't figure out how. Then, one day, without meaning to, my husband gave me a giant push right into the proverbial oncoming traffic.

Ten years ago, my commonplace life came to a halt when my husband decided to follow his dream to open a restaurant. I had never worked in a restaurant. In fact, I had never worked a retail job in my life. But, this was my husband's dream, so I told him I'd help for a bit. My first big responsibility was hiring our crew. With absolutely zero experience, I interviewed twenty-two individuals. Because I was too afraid to turn anyone down, I hired every single candidate to become my crew of mostly inexperienced kids.

The day we opened, I had to take an order at the register. It was difficult to hear the customer's order over the jack-hammering of my heart. I quickly learned to work in the kitchen to avoid having to greet new customers. Unfortunately, hiding out didn't last too long. We had opened a 5000 square foot store in an undeveloped neighborhood, right at the beginning of the worst housing crash in history. We had only a third of the population we had expected. My husband kept his day job, so we had some extra income to make ends meet. Initially, he worked from the store. He would take calls for his day job as needed while handling the business finances. I worked in the kitchen all day, picked the kids up from school, and returned to help in the evenings. We had a cot in the office so our youngest could nap, and occasionally my husband would stay the night. Then summer came around. We had no extra money to pay for childcare, and someone had to stay home with the kids. There was no way my husband could work his day job and manage the store by himself, so he stayed home with the kids. I had a crash course in managing the store. Due to limited funds for staffing, I was also forced to bartend, the worst job imaginable for this chicken.

Day after day, I pretended that I was outgoing, cheerfully greeting customers, yet feeling so insecure wondering what to say, and dying inside if there was ever an awkward pause. With no hope of the store improving any time soon, I had become a chicken frozen in the fast lane fearfully dodging the cars of life whizzing by me.

We struggled through the first few years, and just when I thought things were beginning to turn for the better, they turned for the worse.

It's never a good thing when someone walks into a restaurant with a clipboard and a suit, but that's exactly what happened one day. This lady, with her stiff Aqua-net curled hair, polyester gray pant-suit, and sensible black shoes, curtly introduced herself. She flipped through some papers from her clipboard and handed me a notice from the department of taxation. It was a cease and desist notice if we didn't make arrangements to pay our delinquent sales tax. I stared in disbelief. The letter stated that sales tax hadn't been paid in months. My eyes scanned the letter trying to make sense of it. This had to be a mistake. I thought we were almost out of the woods, and I was just handed a delinquency notice for *eighty thousand* dollars. My heart was pounding out of my chest, and my stomach clenched into a knot. I didn't know what to say, and her demeanor was not helping my anxiety. All I could think was, this can't be right. "Let me call my husband," was all I could cluck. My hands shook as I dialed his number, my voice raising in disbelief as I recounted the situation. He confirmed it was correct and told me he'd handle it. How is he so fricking calm? Somehow, as my throat was tightening to a close, I assured her that we'd take care of it. My mind was reeling, tears stung my eyes, and a feeling of anger seethed through me as my resentment for the business, and for my husband, took hold. Miraculously, with the help of our timely income tax return, a series of work bonuses, and a high-interest/short-term loan, my husband was able to put together a payment plan, and we were not shut down. The next several months we managed to cut back even more. Whew! A close call to keep a business I now hated. He reassured me everything was all good—and I mistakenly believed him.

Day after day, we struggled on, and the pit in my stomach did not go away. I decided to work towards getting more organized, hoping it would reduce my constant anxiety. On one of my husband's business trips, I decided I would catch up on filing paperwork in his office. I brought out bags of papers to sort through, and, as I discovered that my husband had six months of unopened mail, a sinking feeling set in. As I opened each late notice, I slowly started to realize he had stopped paying mortgages for all of our rentals. The anger began to boil as I also discovered unopened checks that would have come in handy on countless occasions. Ironically, while I was tearing open notice after notice, the doorbell rang, and I was handed our first notice of foreclosure. My hatred for the restaurant grew, and a similar feeling was emerging for my husband. My mind desperately told me to run back to safety, get out of the business, and while I was at it, leave my marriage. I started looking for a job and apartments. I spent hours escaping reality each day on Facebook, cyber-stalking friends I no longer had due to investing all my time into the business. How did everything become such a mess?! Depression took hold, and I went through the motions doing what I had to do while retreating back to my phone every chance I could get. I hated my life.

While contemplating divorce and reeling over our financial disaster, I got a call from my daughter's school to pick her up because she wasn't feeling well. She was twelve at the time and always complained about not feeling well. I got her home and was a bit ticked because she didn't even have a fever. I was not very patient with her, but let her spend the rest of the day sleeping. I went back to manage our store and continued my quest to organize the chaos around me, right down to emptying the lost and found bin. Most items were going to Goodwill, except for a tattered book called *The Power* by Rhonda Byrne, who also wrote *The Secret*. I had heard about *The Secret*, and, at this point, I figured I could use all the help I could get. All I needed was to find some time to read—a pastime for personal growth that I had given up long ago.

The next morning, my daughter's temperature had risen to 106 Fahrenheit. I made a not so great parenting decision and attempted to keep the fever down with ibuprofen for the next three days. Unfortunately, the fever kept spiking, and I finally arranged for someone else to manage the store and took my daughter to the hospital. They immediately hooked her up to an

IV, started with blood tests, and admitted her overnight to keep watch and run more tests. The next day's chest x-rays revealed cavities were forming in her lungs. I was informed that she would not be leaving the hospital anytime soon. While she slept, I ran home to grab a few items so I could stay at the hospital with her, and figured I might find some reading time after all. So, I brought my 'new' book. Between the daily tests, doctors' consultations, and fearful thoughts that I could lose my daughter, I had plenty of time to read and reflect. With each page I read, I was encouraged to think about the things I loved in a life I hated. Of course, I began thinking of all the things I loved about my daughter. I desperately wanted to hear her sing again, since that was her passion. I didn't care about the school she was missing or her grades. I stopped worrying about our finances and the accruing medical bills. I just wanted to see her happy. I just wanted my family to remain intact.

It took a week in the hospital for my daughter to finally be diagnosed with a potentially deadly septic staph infection. Six weeks of intravenous antibiotics, and countless numbers of follow up visits later, we were able to celebrate my daughter's recovery. This was the most horrific ordeal of my life, and it completely changed my perspective. If it weren't for living through this nightmare with my daughter and having time to read the book that mysteriously appeared in my lost and found, I'm not sure I would have gotten through those years with my business and marriage intact. At that point, I felt like I had been hit by a semi, and whirling from the blow I had come to a crossroads. I realized I could either go back to a safe, boring life by leaving my husband, or be thankful for what I have, keep moving forward, and celebrate each adventurous moment I have with my family. The gratitude I was feeling for my family being intact had given me the courage to take the next couple of steps.

As I reread my new favorite book, I realized my husband, the person I resented most, was my best friend. I recalled the feelings I had while holding hands on our first date, the joy I had when we got engaged, the raw emotion while reciting our wedding vows, and all the wonderful moments we've shared through the years. The reality was my husband could always make me smile and laugh, even through our financial crisis. I stopped resenting him for a second and realized he needed my help. I was blaming him for our circumstances, and at that point, I realized that if I didn't like how things were going, I was the only one responsible for changing them. I learned how to use budgeting software, took over the finances for the business, and created a budgeting system to make sure the bills got paid. I insisted that we work as a team and communicate to find solutions together. It seemed that almost immediately, we stopped bleeding out money.

I began watching motivational videos and reading more self-help books which led me to do more of what I enjoyed and less blaming of my husband for our circumstances. I realized that I had always wanted to travel and decided to schedule family trips instead of hunting for Christmas gifts no one really needed. I worked on my own development in health, fitness, and creative pursuits. I stopped worrying so much about my kids' grades and focused on having fun. Things were continuously improving. My feelings of self-loathing were diminishing, but there was a piece of me still not feeling fulfilled.

That was until I read another book, but this one was about dreaming big. My *big* dream would be to change the education system. I wasn't sure how, but I decided that was what I was going to do. Aside from my family, education was my passion and had been missing from my life. I got up the guts to get involved in some networking groups and met women excited to be following their dreams. I joined an online personal development group and truly stepped out of my comfort zone. For the first time in my life, I went on a trip by myself. I traveled to Chicago to meet the founders of the personal development group that I had seen years ago on *Oprah*. Although shaking uncontrollably, I shared my education idea with them. To my amazement, I was later contacted by one of the founders of the event to collaborate. The validation I felt was huge. While it didn't go anywhere, she liked what I had to say, and it gave me some courage to keep moving forward. I had crossed another lane on my life's highway.

I started attending women's conferences, surrounding myself with people building their dream and pushing through their own obstacles. They were all ahead of me—or so it seemed—and my familiar fear returned. I mean, I didn't even have a business name for my education program! I struggled with moving forward, but I had already shared my idea with so many. Ironically, now I was too chicken to turn back.

I was still riding the high from my first solo trip, so I traveled to another conference on my own. I awkwardly sat with people I didn't know, pretending it didn't bother me. At one point, I was brought to tears as I listened to a powerhouse of a woman tell her story. It was my story. Shy, struggling with depression, pushing through and now speaking to hundreds. She seemed to have it all together. She was just like me, except she was no longer a chicken. She had actually reached the other side, and all of the women at the event were supporting her. I wondered if I'd ever get to be like that? As I engaged with some of the women there, I was repeatedly told how brave I was to be there on my own. I was asked if I was part of leadership. I was told I was not awkward. A thought crept into my mind that maybe I'm not the person I've always thought I was. The fear I had earlier was beginning to turn in to excitement.

As I continued to dive into personal and professional development books and classes, things really started to turn around. My marriage had become stronger as we worked to improve our communication and I stopped hating our business. Through my new practice of daily gratitude, I began to love what I had learned from the business and became grateful I hadn't walked away. The business and all its challenges had made me stronger, and my search for fulfillment was what had led me to the pursuit of MY dream. With all the encouragement I had been receiving from my networking groups, I considered becoming a managing director for one of them to build my leadership skills. I hemmed and hawed, and someone beat me to it. I told myself I couldn't have done it anyway.

Yet, practically the next day, another networking group announced that they needed a managing director. Was this a sign? I took it as one and applied. Terrified. But, I finally committed to stop hiding behind my phone and staying in the shadows. I started enjoying where I was. Once again, my fear was turning into excitement.

Then, just like that, I became a managing director of a women's group. My gratitude for surviving the previous lanes was growing, and I was learning how to navigate more boldly. I had begun to take charge of my life and had stepped into the next lane by my own choice. I realized that I was completely in charge of my life, so how do I want it to turn out?

Further reflection made me realize the power I had within me to change my life for the better. I was losing my business, so I learned how to run a business. My marriage lacked communication, so we started talking. I had no friends, so I surrounded myself with people looking to make friends. I was shy and quiet, so I joined a public speaking group. I joined a self-help book club and met with other women looking to encourage each other and grow personally and professionally.

Recently, I realized I was actually feeling happy about myself. Not because things are perfect, but because I was learning and growing. I wasn't following anyone else's prescription. I wasn't doing it for money. I wasn't trying to impress anyone. I wasn't even doing it for my family. Fear or no fear, I was doing it for myself. I was putting one chicken leg in front of the other and crossing the damned road on my own, with lots of encouragement from the people around me, and learning from each and every obstacle.

As I continue to overcome the horrible things I thought about myself, I have become grateful for the struggles I've had personally, financially, and with my relationships that have taught me how to overcome life's obstacles. Getting knocked down isn't failing unless you decide to not get back up. I will always get back up, and I've learned that my obstacles only make me stronger. I don't fail. I just figure things out. I have learned that every challenge I had was bringing me closer to being truly happy. I have determined that my life, as boring as I have always thought it to be, has turned into a grand adventure, and deserves to be shared.

Today, I have reached the other side of the road, as I discovered my dream of creating an education center. As I look around, I think the grass may actually be greener over here, or maybe it's just that I learned about the power of gratitude. I'm pretty sure I see another road ahead, which is okay as I'm no longer a chicken. During my internal transformation, I realized that I'm actually an eagle, no longer alone on my journey. With those encouraging me, including my own thoughts, I am rising up, soaring across the roads ahead of me.

Laura Watson

Laura Watson received her Bachelor's in Child Development, Master's in Education and taught for eighteen years. She left teaching to raise her children, and later became the owner/ operator of her husband's dream restaurant. Together, they have just celebrated ten years of business, and twenty-four years of marriage.

Today, Laura is an active volunteer in her community and uses the family business to support youth sports and education initiatives. She is continuing her passion for learning by participating in ongoing personal and professional development activities. Currently, she is furthering her leadership skills as the managing director of a women's networking group, writing her first book, and pursuing her own dream of opening an alternative education center. She is dedicating this book to her family and to those that haven't yet written their story.

Not Your Typical Statistic

By Angie Garcia

My story starts as far back as I can remember.

I was six years old and was migrating from Mexico City to Reno, NV. I didn't cross a massive river, nor did I trek a hot desert. I left on a bus with my mom and my younger sister. I walked through what I now know was customs, arm in hand with my uncle. There was a lot of secrecy upon arrival at my aunt's house, but there was also the joy of reuniting with family members.

I have a better understanding of exactly what that secrecy was as an adult. My mom and I were undocumented; we had immigrated illegally and were staying with other family members who were also undocumented.

I remember staying with different groups of family members until my dad was able to save up for a place of our own. Cramped spaces and the feeling of not having anything to call my own overwhelmed me. We only had the clothes on our backs and a few small bags of personal items.

While the living situation was cramped, the family members we stayed with were more than welcoming. Good food, great music, and lots of laughter made the living situations a lot easier. Aunts, uncles, grandparents, cousins, and godparents were our constant support. I will always admire that about my family—their willingness to help each other during difficult times and find the ability to laugh about the fucked-up-ness that was our lives.

As an undocumented immigrant family, we had to find our circle of support quickly if we wanted to not only survive but also thrive in a new country.

While the thought of attending school in a different country and learning a different language was intimidating, I was excited and eager to start. I attended an ESL program where I soaked up every English word like a sponge. I was that bubbly little girl who asked a lot of questions and made friends easily, which made learning the language that much easier.

We lived near a street called Montello. In the early 90's, Montello Street was an area of town with a lot of illegal gang activity. My parents were very protective of me and my sister, so we weren't allowed to go out much. I remember gunshots and sirens at night, and an incident where my mom ran out to cover a naked, battered female while my dad chased off her abuser. It's something that traumatizes the mind of an eight-year-old child.

Don't get me wrong; my neighborhood wasn't *all* horrible. The families there rallied together and looked out for one another. I had neighbors that would lend us a cup of sugar for lemonade and kept an eye on us kids while we played. I have always been able to see the good in bad situations, even as a child.

While certain events traumatized me, I took away the pride I felt for my parents for doing the right thing. My parents have always answered the call to serve others. In Spanish, there is a word for that pride; it's called *servicial*. This word is used to describe a person who serves. They always volunteered in church and helped out our community. I love and admire them for instilling that in me.

While I love both of my parents, I have always been really close to my dad. I was definitely a daddy's girl. When I was little, I would tell my dad I wanted to be a boy. I knew how badly my dad wanted a son, but as much as I tried to do 'boy things' with him, he would always put me in my place. My role was in the kitchen, cleaning and helping my mom with my siblings.

My sister, Michelle, was my resilience during those difficult years. Her companionship, support, and love are what got me through some very tough times. It was just her and me for seven years, before my other four siblings were born, which made us inseparable.

We witnessed my father's alcoholism turn into violence towards my mother and did our best to shield our younger siblings from having to witness it. We endured what our parents called 'financial hardships', which I now know was more like extreme poverty.

There were many times where we had to stretch rice, beans, milk, and eggs provided by WIC (Women, Infants, and Children government assistance) for days until food stamps kicked in. There were times where we were forced to move in with family, and all of us would stay in one bedroom. Times were definitely difficult.

My sister and I became my mother's constant support during my dad's absence. I found out at a very young age my dad had a drinking problem. I loved that man, but I began to feel hate towards him. He spent a large portion of my childhood and adolescence in and out of jail due to DUIs. I could *never* understand why my mom would always take him back. She seemed so strong and independent when he was away, but the minute he returned, she became this fragile, anxious person I began to resent.

I look back now on the entire situation, and my heart hurts for her. This was a broken, undocumented, hard-working mother of six with no family of her own nearby. The only family she had was my dad's family.

While I resented her, I always did my best to help her out. When I turned fourteen, while my friends were all looking for summer jobs, I came to the realization that I was not able to work legally. I was confused at first and became angry and hurt. My sense of belonging was shattered, and my feeling of self-worth was gone. I always felt like an American, a true Nevadan at heart, but at the end of the day, I was an undocumented Mexican (or how others so hurtfully put it, "an illegal").

I had entered the U.S. illegally. Therefore I was unable to obtain a social security card, much less a Nevada ID. I began to resent my mom and dad. I blamed them for my legal status instead of realizing they brought me to the U.S. in the hopes of a better life. I wish I could have seen the positive side of that situation. I was, after all, in the U.S., the land of opportunity.

Unfortunately, I was a moody teenager dealing with abnormally difficult circumstances. I had no social life, I took care of my siblings, and I helped my mom when she left for work (which I had been doing since the tender age of nine). I remember always having to flake on my friends.

I loved my little brothers and sisters, and I never resented them. I took the role of big sister very seriously. I remember wanting to be a good role model for them. My grades were always good, and my love for school continued to grow.

I remember coming home one day with my report card, beaming! I had straight A's, except for one B in science. I was never good at science—it just went in one ear and out the other. So to get a B in that subject was pretty impressive, in my opinion. I showed my dad my card, and his response was, "What is that? Show me once you have straight A's". I felt so hurt by not receiving some form of appreciation for all I did or recognition for my hard work, in school and at home.

I was a good daughter, I had no social life aside from church youth groups and always maintained good grades until I began to rebel around the age of fifteen. Suddenly, I found myself hanging out with the wrong crowd at school. I would ditch to go drinking with friends and began to truly believe there was no point in trying so hard. I was undocumented and, sadly, a high school diploma wasn't going to change that.

A month before my sixteenth birthday, I met my best friend, Carlos. I felt so alone in the world at that time. He understood what it felt like to be broken and how it felt when society had given up on you. He was a high school dropout and former gang member trying to do right by someone. All I desperately needed was to feel loved and appreciated.

The relationship between my parents and me became unbearable. I had called the cops on my dad after a physical altercation he had with my mom, and he was incarcerated. When he got out of jail, my mom allowed him back home, and he made it very clear that he resented me for what happened. I felt horrible having to leave my siblings behind, but I couldn't take it anymore.

I found out I was pregnant and decided to leave. I moved in with Carlos and ended up dropping out of high school. We were two young, dumb, and broke kids in love who only had each other. I was unable to work due to my legal status, and as a high school dropout, Carlos struggled to find a good paying job.

I was living with so much guilt at that time. I felt guilty for turning my back on my siblings, for getting pregnant so young, for making so many stupid decisions.

I decided to reach out for help and apply for government assistance. There I was in line at the welfare office, undocumented, eighteen years old with my little girl, and I felt like a typical statistic. Whom did this child have to look up to? What chances did she have to make it in this world if her parents could barely get by?

While it was a low point in my life, I'm grateful I had help. Unfortunately, I would not qualify for assistance due to my legal status, but my little girl could.

In March of 2008, after my third daughter's birth, Carlos was laid off from his job. It felt like the rug got pulled from under us. We were finally making ends meet and starting to get our lives together. As I brought my baby girl home from the hospital, I noticed a flyer on the door of our apartment. We were living in Housing Authority apartments, and the RHA was offering paid training in certain fields. We applied to get help to pay for Carlos to take truck driving classes and receive his CDL. During the interview for the assistance, they asked him why he wanted this training and all he kept saying was, "I just want to get out of housing. I want to be able to make it on my own."

That did it. They awarded him with paid training. Who else was going to just give us $2,500 to do that? It felt like a chance to prove to society we weren't what they thought we were. Two high school dropouts, living off the government—it was not an unlikely story of chance.

After Carlos secured his paid training, everything shifted in our lives. As soon as he started truck driving, we were able to leave housing and make a real effort to make it on our own.

While we were still struggling, things were working out. I was a stay-at-home mom, and I cherished every moment of it. During my oldest daughter's kindergarten graduation, she asked me what year I had graduated high school. I didn't have the heart to tell her I hadn't graduated, so I made the decision to enroll in an alternative high school. I was guided by staff who went above and beyond their job description. They took care of my three daughters while I tested for my GED to waive credits. This same staff stood outside with my children and entertained them while I took my Nevada proficiency exams. They never once made me feel like a horrible student when I didn't turn something in or fell off the face of the earth.

In June 2009, I received my adult high school diploma from Washoe High School. I decided to speak during my graduation and let my voice be heard.

While my knees shook, and my voice cracked, I spoke of the feelings of failure and second chances. I thanked the staff that provided unconditional support to an undocumented teen mom who needed a chance to prove herself worthy.

It felt amazing; I had a taste of success and felt so incredibly accomplished.

While I had graduated high school, I was still undocumented. Instead of feeling sorry for myself, I volunteered at my kid's school. I volunteered during a program my mom coordinated through the school district called Familias Unidas, or United Families in English. This program had weekly meetings for Spanish-speaking parents to help them become more involved in their kids' school. I would take my daughter and my newborn son and provide child care for other parents. I assisted families with translation, application assistance for welfare, and location of resources in the community for basic needs. I felt useful, and, for the first time in a long time, I didn't feel like a failure.

In 2012, the Obama administration founded the DACA (Deferred Action for Childhood Arrivals) immigration policy. DACA allowed certain undocumented immigrants who entered the country as minors to receive a renewable two-year period of deferred action from deportation and eligibility for a work permit.

Of course I was scared and hesitant to apply for the program; it felt like a trap. It took my husband about a year to save up $1,000 and me to summon the courage to *finally* apply.

I was tired of feeling stuck, of feeling like a burden to my husband. We were fighting so much, and money was always so tight. In 2014, I received my two-year work permit. I hit the ground running and applied for work, but with little-to-no experience, the jobs I was finding just didn't seem right. I found a call center job, but the hours were horrible. I felt like I never saw my children, and the calls were so stressful.

Something inside me was telling me I was meant for something else—my empathy and ability to problem solve was needed elsewhere. I felt like I was meant to be in a position where I could help others. Friends suggested I apply for the school district. All I kept thinking was go big or go home Angie!

While searching for openings, I spotted a family advocate position. I applied and submitted my very short resume, about half a page. I had volunteer experience, experience as a front desk attendant at my aunt's dry cleaners, and a very short time at the call center. I was shocked when I received a call for an interview.

The day of my interview, my anxiety peaked. It was a three-panel interview, which made it even more stressful, but the moment I sat down, something told me this was my job.

I was meant to be there, and I owned it.

I smiled and answered all of the questions with confidence. About four days later, I received a call back telling me I was successful.

In this position, I have met some amazing women. I call them my lady tribe. I met my boss, Brenda, who gave this DACA recipient an opportunity to prove herself. She has been my mentor and my confidant. Her mentorship has given me the opportunity to envision a better life for myself and has empowered me to go after my dreams. To have a boss that understands what it's like to be a working mother and a wife, a boss who not only encourages you to do amazing things but brags about the amazing things you do, is truly humbling.

I have met other amazing women—like Nellie—a badass single mom who was willing to go above and beyond for me. When I was unable to find a sponsor during my naturalization process, she stepped up and did what very few were willing to do. Thanks to her and my husband, I am a legal resident of the United States. I have met so many other amazing and empowering females in this job.

Females that have encouraged me to continue learning.

Females that push me to celebrate, care for, and love myself.

Females that give me a reason to laugh during those days when I feel like I can't even breathe.

I am a firm believer that healed women heal women. Every female needs a lady tribe, a group of females that have your back and empower you to be a better version of yourself. Surround yourself with happy people that wish you happiness, and you *will* succeed.

In February 2016, my dad passed away. He was returning from a trip to Mexico with other family members. While crossing New Mexico, the vehicle they were in rolled over on the highway during a snowstorm. My grandma and great aunt were severely injured and taken to the ICU in Dallas, Texas. My godmother had a broken leg, and my father passed away instantly.

I never knew I could feel such pain. It was a gut-wrenching, heart-stabbing pain. My dad had been sober for twelve years and had completely turned his life around. He was a devoted, hard-working father and would help anyone in need.

I had forgiven my father long ago; nothing was left unsaid. He was my go-to guy for everything. We were starting to become close again, which made his absence hurt that much more. To my kids, he was Papi Chava, and to see them hurt and cry when I broke the news was one of the most difficult things I've ever had to do.

His death broke me, but it also changed me. It taught me that I need to live my life the way I want to live it, without fear of the unknown.

So, I decided to jump.

To do all those things that scare me.

To write my goals, plan them, and then crush them.

To enroll in college (I start in the fall). I hope to obtain my social work degree to better help others.

I decided to take the opportunity to write my story in hopes that someone reads it and chooses to jump as well. Maybe someone else will feel the power behind not being tied down or being a victim of their past. I have been the underdog many times throughout my life, and at times I truly felt like a typical statistic.

Sadly, I allowed depression and anxiety to reign over me for far too long.

I allowed negativity to creep into my life, and I distanced myself from people who loved me.

I allowed self-sabotage and fear to hold me back and denied myself of self-love. I didn't see what others saw in me or why others considered me to be special.

There were many days where I felt broken due to crappy choices and circumstances. Perseverance during those difficult days and mustering up the will to show up, surrounding myself with the right people, and a bit of grit and positivity has allowed me to create my own comeback story and find the courage to share it with others.

This is my comeback story. Flawed, chaotic and messy, yet beautiful, empowering and filled with achievements. Don't ever feel shame for reaching out for help, whether it's parenting classes, applying for welfare or accepting support from other women. If you're currently at a low point in your life, just remember your story is waiting to be written. Reach out for help to get to the point where you can write your own comeback story.

Angie Garcia

Angelica Garcia, known by family and friends as Angie, is a thirty-year old married mother of three beautiful, strong willed girls and one rambunctious little boy.

Born in Mexico, Angie moved to Nevada as a young girl. She considers herself a true Nevadan at heart. Angie holds a position as a family advocate and parenting facilitator for the Washoe County School District's Family Resource Centers. Her position has allowed her to give back to the community in ways she never imagined. Helping low income families have a voice in their community is something she believes strongly in. Having been in similar situations herself, she believes that every person deserves dignity and respect, and works diligently to provide that for the people she meets.

Broken-Hearted

By Nicole Howell

It's two o'clock in the morning, and I'm lying on this cold, plastic, squeaky, uncomfortable hospital bed gazing out the wide windows upon the city I grew up in. Snow quietly blanketing the sleepy valley floor, streetlights gently illuminate the silent byways. How did I get here? How is this possible? How is this my life? Hours ago, I was sitting at my dinner table reconnecting over steak, salad, and vodka with an old friend I had been estranged from for a decade. I had been downplaying the extreme tightening in my chest, chalking it up to anxiety. *Just take another drink and try to be present for your friend*, I told myself. *She is in need and sharing so openly about the years of her struggle that I was not there to witness. She's really opening up about what's gone on. Why is this tightness lasting so long? Why won't this anxiety let up?* I take a deep breath, but that makes it worse. My heart beats so hard in my chest I cannot even hear her speaking. *Just be present with your friend*, I tell myself.

My friend had her troubles to share, but so did I. As we spoke, she admitted she had known things; things she thought I knew, things you don't tell your friends less you risk losing them. It's no surprise that there's a tightening. She understands, she says, but I still don't. I still don't understand how my marriage of twenty-five years failed. My marriage, that I thought defied the odds: the odds of getting married too young, succeeding inside of a law-enforcement career. We were the exception to the rule, I thought. My husband, who sent me twenty texts a day telling me he loved me, telling me he was just thinking of me, we were the exception to the rule. We had the best sex life of any couple I knew! But I was wrong. I was wrong in a big way. I was wrong in a way that makes you want to put your hand to your heart and gasp in disbelief. My friend says she understands that, but sometimes I still don't. As I walked her to the door, we say our goodbyes, my chest is still so tight, and now there's a knot in my throat. *It will pass, it's understandable with what I'm going through*, I think. I close the door. I take a deep breath, now even more concerned that it has been unabated for almost three hours. *This will pass*, I think. *Go take a bath, go to bed.* As I climb the stairs, it's harder and harder to catch my breath. I'm getting more and more scared. This has got to be anxiety, I think.

The man I relied on for almost thirty years is not here. I'm on my own. If I just get to bed, everything will be okay. As I reach the top of the stairs, I begin to have a sickening feeling that something is really wrong. My legs feel suddenly weaker. I begin to cry and don't know what to do. Do I turn to my left, go to my empty bedroom and cry myself to sleep again like I've done so many nights in the last couple of weeks, or do I turn right and wake my daughter to ask her for help? How could this be happening? I walk slowly to the right, tears quickening, and as I open her bedroom door I whisper "Ali, Ali, honey I think there's something really wrong." She immediately springs from bed towards me. I walk past her room to the bathroom and collapse on the floor. My sweet girl, only eighteen, had been learning about sports medicine in high school, so she knew to take my pulse, she knew to take my blood pressure, she knew to keep calm, but she didn't know how to handle the sobbing. "I'm going to throw up," I tell her. "I don't know what's wrong baby, but I think we need to go to the hospital." The next twenty minutes is a blur as we drive the seven miles to the hospital. I lose consciousness three times. I can hear Ali talking to the 911 operator as I say, "Don't stop baby, just keep driving." I hear her shaky voice tell the 911 operator that her mom lost consciousness again, and again I mumble, "Keep driving baby, we're almost there you're doing so great." As we pull into the emergency room bay of the hospital, she sprints from the car.

Inside the doors she shouts, "Someone, please come help my mom." Several staff members rush out and gently help me onto a gurney. The tightness in my chest seems to subside a little as I get a chest X-ray and blood is drawn. *I overreacted. I don't know how to do this by myself, I don't know how to do hard things by myself, I've never had to.* My husband had moved out of our home less than two weeks ago, but I needed him by my side now. "Ali, call your dad, tell him I'm in the hospital, ask him to come," There were several interviews by hospital staff asking me what happened. "When did you start feeling the tightness? How long did it last? Why did you wait three hours? Has is this ever happened before?"

My husband entered through the curtain wall. His once loving and gentle gaze was now cold, distant and notably emotionally disconnected. "What happened?" he asks. "You're just dehydrated," he diagnosed. *He's right,* I think. *Night after night of crying myself to sleep, I let myself get dehydrated, that's all. I have overreacted and upset everybody.* As the doctor and a nurse entered, they opened the curtain wide revealing the nurse's station behind them. *Oh God, I'm an idiot.*

"Nicole, you're having a heart attack," the doctor pronounced. "That's not possible, I'm forty-four," I rebutted. "Well it's happening," the doctor stated, very matter of fact. My attention turned to my husband, stone-faced. He would not return my gaze. I looked at my daughter, and we traded concerned, loving glances. She feels the same disbelief that I do, like how can this be? "What happens now?" my husband asks. "We're going to admit her to the cardiac unit continue to monitor her levels to make sure that they don't get any worse." He continues talking about their course of action, x-rays, stress test, heart enzyme levels. I can barely hear, and I definitely cannot focus on what he's saying. How could any of this actually be happening?

My eyes turned back to the snow falling over the valley, I can see the high school that I attended, I can see the road that I first learned to drive a car on. I can see the police department that was such a big part of my marriage. For twenty-five years it was the 'other woman' in our marriage. I thought it was the only 'other woman'. We had arrived at the hospital around 9 p.m.; my friends all started arriving about 11p.m. My husband had come with me from the ER to the cardiac unit. I wanted him by my side, but as my friends arrived, he quickly chose to leave. "Stay," I urged. "Nik, they all hate me", he rebutted. "I need to go and let them be here for you." I asked him to check in on our daughter Bella. We had not even woken her when we left, as to not terrify her. He agreed and left. I sent Ali home. "I'll be fine until morning," I promised. My friends bombarded me with questions, one after another. "How could you have a heart attack? Now what happens? What's next?" I don't really know the answers to any of the questions. Each time they check my heart enzymes levels, they continue to rise. Who knew a heart attack lasted hours?

By midnight it was quiet, the joking and laughter left, and my brain starts playing out every possible scenario. My kids are still reeling from the final separation of their parents. There had been three separations before, only one the kids actually knew about. This was the final one, and the kids are mad, really mad at their dad. What happens if I die? My girls will never forgive their dad; they will be ruined forever. He'll never forgive himself! I was overwhelmed by the horror of the situation. All I could think to do was move all the wires and monitors coming off my body to one side, slide out of bed to my knees and pray. I haven't prayed on my knees in at least fifteen years. "Please Lord, please let me stay here and raise my girls. I can handle anything else if you'll just let me raise my babies!" Tears stream down my face. I crawl back into my bed, still in shock by the events of the day. I stared out into the snowy night and cried myself to sleep.

The last several years were filled with revelations and admissions of adultery. The story started with a lap dance that turned into a one-night stand, to explaining why I needed to get a chlamydia test after twenty-one years of marriage, and ended four years later with the admission of chronic infidelity over our entire relationship. As the story unfolded over the years, I made excuses and took him back. *I love him, he loves me,* I told myself. *We made a family, we can make it work. His job is unbelievably stressful, he has PTSD not only from work but from his own parents' divorce. It's not his fault,* I reasoned. *He has to constantly be hyper-vigilant, his serotonin is bottomed out, this is just thrill-seeking behavior, it can be corrected,* I hoped. We are the family who gets through the hard stuff. We taught a class at the police department on surviving the impact of critical incidents. After years of lies on top of lies, the crazed, manic letters from his ex-girlfriend and another woman's ex-husband's letter, it all became unbearable. In the midst of learning the shocking truths and trying to piece my marriage back together again and again for four years, I chose to take on my personal growth and learned the most valuable lesson of my life. I saw how fear kept me in a marriage that clearly didn't work. How fear had me make excuses for his behavior. It was the fear of being on my own, fear of taking care of my kids alone, fear of how I would financially support myself, fear of not being with the man who was my best friend for almost thirty years. Once I faced the fear, I moved past it, and I realized that all that was left was for me to make a powerful choice. I chose to get divorced.

Once the fear was gone, all that remained was the choice to create a life of my own design. I finally called it quits just before Thanksgiving. Not because I couldn't forgive him, but because he couldn't forgive himself; well, at least that's what I told myself. I lay in the hospital on December 7, and I realized it was more than my heart could take. The next morning involved hours of testing; stress tests, blood draws and still no answers. My enzyme levels finally stopped climbing about 9 a.m. but I still no real answers as to what caused the heart attack. I never did receive answers. The only thing that made sense was discussed at a follow-up visit weeks later, takotsubo—broken-heart syndrome. When my primary doc suggested it, a knot tightened in my throat and tears rolled down my face. "Yes… that's what it is… I am completely broken-hearted."

Broken-hearted or not, I get to choose how I show up in life:

I choose how I talk to my ex-husband.

I choose how I talk to my kids.

I choose how to medicate my pain.

I laid down some ground rules: no drinking at home by myself, limit Xanax to complete meltdowns, no bashing the ex to the kids, and no hateful words that I can never take back.

We had put the house on the market right after our separation in November and had an offer the first week of December. We were set to close January 17. We just had to get through Christmas and find a new place to live. I looked at everything in our neighborhood and hated it. After a trip to the local grocery store where I had to explain to yet another mutual friend that we were getting divorced, I thought, *I've got to get the hell out of this neighborhood.* It's not a big town, but I knew moving to the other side would mean a whole new life and no more depressing grocery run-ins.

At first, I didn't want to move the kids away from their school, but as we started to look at other areas, we all started getting excited about a new start in a cool and hip part of town. I have two close friends who live in the historic district in Reno. I had always been in love with their houses and dreamed of someday being able to move there. Lo and behold, my friend's neighbor was moving out, and I was moving in. We called our places the Healing Houses. I remained broken-hearted for a long time, but I keep reminding myself that I get to choose. I get to choose how I show up every day, the words that I say, and the actions that I take. I never imagined a life without my husband. I moved from my mom's house into his. We started dating when I was sixteen, and we got married the week before I turned nineteen; he was twenty-three. I knew that we were young, but we were ready to take on the world. Six years in we bought our first home, and a year later we had Alicia; three years later we were blessed with another beautiful girl, Isabella. House first, then babies. These were his rules, but I was thankful for them.

I started to make all the rules. It was uncomfortable, but doing so allowed me to remember the girl I was before I was my husband's wife. The next sixteen months of my life changed everything. I had left the family businesses I ran with the ex, and I went back to work in interior design. I began what felt like a million firsts.

- First time dating as an adult

- First time sleeping with someone else

- First time negotiating an employment contract and excepting a career position without my husband's advice

- First time to make a very hard decision and leave the best paying job I'd ever had but could not stand.

- Starting my own design firm

- Signing a very expensive commercial lease

- Co-creating a movement to empower female entrepreneurs

There were many times my natural inclination to text my husband crept in. Sometimes I could not stop myself; it always fell on deaf ears, but fear no longer ran my life—possibility did.

Inside of my personal and professional development, I attended a weekend course where the crescendo was creating, with the other participants, a new possibility for our lives. I was thrilled to just open my mouth and see what would fall out. I stood nervously in the front of the room and said, "The possibility I am creating for myself and my life is the possibility… of grace, vulnerability, love."

What? Who said those words? Where did that come from? Grace? Like, from God? Where did that come from?

Outside of praying for my life, I was not a religious woman. I powerfully stated those possibilities as ways of being in my life, and as soon as I got to my seat, I leaned over to my partner that I had had for the last three days and whispered, one eyebrow raised high and shoulders shrugged, "Grace?" Where did that come from?" I asked. "Nicole," he whispered back, "that's who you are for people, that's who you've been for me all week long, and that's who you are for your ex-husband." His comment landed with a thud on my heart.

Grace, vulnerability, love. Those words would be my mantra. It became my answer to everything.

Who am I when:

The kids have hard questions about their dad?
Grace, vulnerability, love.
When the fear of taking on a business and lease that's as much as the rent at my house?
Grace, vulnerability, love.
When I give my heart too easily in a new relationship and get hurt, disappointed, rejected?
Grace, vulnerability, love.

When I'm scared of how BIG I'm being and what I'm willing to take on.

Grace, vulnerability, love.

When I want to crush my ex-husband.

Grace, vulnerability, love.

When I don't want to share my story, and I want to hide.

Grace, vulnerability, love.

When I want to protect my heart from ever being hurt again.

Grace, vulnerability, love.

When I'm called to be so much bigger than I've ever known myself to be, and chase a dream to co-create a women's entrepreneurial center.

Grace, vulnerability, love.

When I'm terrified to tell my story.

Grace, vulnerability, love.

Two and a half years after my hospital stay, I sit in my gorgeous historic home, snuggled under the blankets of my bed in the dark. My iPhone screen illuminates my face that it's 5:09 a.m. I'm writing this story— *my* story— and I know...like I know...like I *know* that this is important. That my message of heartbreak, possibility, and persistence will resonate. It's a call to action my dear friends. I'm speaking to your greatness, to your perfection, to your humanity. Know that you got this. Don't ignore the brave little voice inside yourself. Set your intention and ask for help. Take the fear on. It won't kill you; rather, it will give you more than you ever thought possible.

Nicole Howell

Nicole Howell is the founder and lead designer of Tête Rouge Interiors, a boutique residential interior design firm located in the Inspire Reno building in the historic River Walk District in downtown Reno.

She lives with her daughter Isabella, now sixteen. Her daughter Alicia, now twenty, lives in San Diego California and is pursuing a degree in medicine with a holistic emphasis. This story is dedicated to them. To two amazing girls who, through it all, held their mother's broken heart until she had the strength to take it back. Her story is also dedicated to Landmark Education, where Nicole put her past in the past and stepped into an amazing life she never knew was possible, with grace, vulnerability, and love.

Standing on the Edge

By Pamela Zimmer

I wanted to die.

Standing there at the water's edge—my feet firmly planted in the cold, wet sand. It felt like concrete. I couldn't move. I longed to go into the water.

I wanted to die.

The reflection of the moon and the lights from across the bay made the water look like a giant canyon. It was deep. A cavern. My answer. I thought if I could just take one step into the water, I would fall off the cliff and be gone. My struggles, my anger, my pain…it would all be gone. Yes, my pain. It would disappear. It would dissolve into the deep dark cavern below as I walked into the water.

I wanted to die.

I stood there in the sand for hours. *Literally* hours.

It was New Year's Eve, and what should have been a celebration and happiness with good friends—both new and old—turned into one of the darkest moments of my life. I've had dark moments. This was a turning point. Standing on the water's edge, looking into the reflection.

All I had to do was jump. One step and into the water I would go. To die.

I wanted to die.

Growing up, I was privileged. Not spoiled. Privileged. There is a difference.

We had everything we needed as young girls. We each had our own rooms. We had home cooked meals for dinner every night. We did girl scouts and summer camp. We traveled all over the world, experiencing more culture than most people will in a lifetime.

I say privileged and not spoiled because we still had hand-me-downs. Hand-me-down clothes (especially me, being the younger sister with corduroy pants that had been worn three times before me) and even hand-me-down toys.

I still remember the Barbie camper. Oh, how my sister and I wanted that Barbie camper so badly! We circled it in the Sears catalog at Christmas. We ogled it at our friend's house. We talked about it day and night. It was the one thing as sisters we actually agreed upon.

We finally got it—as a hand-me-down, of course. But, even after getting the one thing we wished for the most, something was still missing. I still felt sad.

When I was ten, I tried to run away.

Like many young pre-teen girls, despite the privileges, I hated my life. I didn't have very many friends, I was constantly teased and called names, and I felt like I just didn't fit in. At home, my older sister and I slayed each other with mean words. "You're adopted, nobody wanted you," I'd taunt. "Well Mom and Dad *chose* me, you were an accident," she'd throw back at me.

I could always count on my mom to encourage me, comfort me, and calmly bandage up a scraped knee or elbow. However, I also remember her being steadfast in executing the rules, discipline, and consequences of our household.

My dad was strict, and when I say strict, I mean super strict. Born as a Jew in Germany during World War II, he escaped to

Switzerland to stay with his aunt until he was finally able to immigrate to the United States with his parents through Ellis Island. I haven't talked to my dad much about his childhood because I don't want to bring that pain up again for him. You can probably imagine the pain he went through and how he deferred and projected some of that pain (unintentionally, I believe) onto my sister and me.

As a little girl, I think I looked up to him. He was strong and had a comfortable lap to sit in for stories and snuggles. I was a "daddy's girl," but as I grew up, I became afraid of him.

He never hit us, aside from the occasional spanking, which in the 70's was totally acceptable and expected. He never abused us in any way. He was simply just stern.

He'd ask questions like:

"What time are you coming home?"
"What time are you doing your homework?"
"How long is your homework going to take you?"

Every day he asked the same questions. They weren't conversation starters. These questions were meant to control every detail of our lives. Strict was an understatement.

I rarely heard my parents say "I love you" to me or my sister. It left me empty, thinking, *does anybody love me?*

Having a 'normal' childhood, you would never think that sadness and depression was something I had to deal with. You might never think that I would want to run away.

But at ten years old, I packed my suitcase, threw it out my bedroom window and all but climbed up on my desk to go before my mom came into my room and stopped me.

I took it a step further when I was thirteen. By this age, I was cutting myself.

The cross was an obsession of mine. Strangely enough, I find meaning in it now, but as an adolescent who had not yet developed a relationship with Jesus Christ or God, let alone was even open to that, it was just one of those things I couldn't explain.

All part of my story. All part of what makes me who I am today.

Nonetheless, I was obsessed with the cross and started carving it into my left hand, right over top of the patch of freckles next to my thumb that always gave me a feeling of anxiety and self-consciousness. I thought if I could carve them away I might be a little more 'normal', accepted, liked, and included. I might have more friends.

I also thought that if I gave myself physical pain, the emotional pain might go away. I don't think I knew that at the time. I know it now. I assume that now. I think that's probably what I was subconsciously thinking.

Our mind is a powerful muscle. My mind, though, thought a lot of things.

Age thirteen was also the year we moved back from living two years in France. (Remember: privileged, not spoiled.)

I can look back on several life experiences now and see the beauty in each one. At eleven years old, however, it felt more like punishment. Plucked from the only home I had ever known and taken to a completely foreign country, I felt angry, scared, and alone.

It wasn't at all the romantic adventure of living in Europe the way you might imagine.

Like me, my mom didn't want to go. In fact, it was two or three years prior from when we actually went that my dad was first asked to move oversees for a new position. My mom had a nervous breakdown, so we didn't go…until later.

Looking back on that particular instance, I find an interesting connection between what I do now and what my mom must have been feeling. I don't know for sure how she felt, but I believe that, like me at the time, there was some part of her that felt lost, empty. Maybe she felt a shift in her identity from woman to wife to mother, giving up her career as a nurse (much like how I gave up my career as an architect) to become a full-time stay-at-home mom.

She never shared much of her emotions, and she never really put herself first, aside from her Friday hair appointments. It's interesting because as much as I wanted to be just like her, I also know how important it is to remember who we are as women, not just as a wife or mother. She was a great mom—the best. Looking back on the past, if I knew then what I know now, I would have told her to take more time for herself. Perhaps that small shift could have made a huge impact in the years that followed.

Mom went to an inpatient facility. It was a mental health hospital (I don't know if I've ever shared that).

I don't remember exactly how long she was there. Other than feeling sad and missing her, I honestly can't remember how I felt about Dad having full responsibility to care for us. All I remember is the smell of the eucalyptus trees that lined the windy road as we drove to visit her after school.

I wish my mom was still alive so I could talk to her about it, and about my own feelings. It's been eleven years since she passed away.

While my mother suffered through some very difficult years of her own, I was suffering through some dark periods too.

As I mentioned, thirteen was tough. The cutting got so bad that I still have a scar on my left hand where I can make out the faint lines of a cross, right over top of the freckles next to my thumb.

Over thirty years later, I still have a scar.

I didn't stop at my hand. The cutting ventured down to my wrist. I can remember when it got that far, the first time I had really thought, *I want to die.*

I didn't have a bad childhood. Nobody hurt me. Nobody abused me. Nobody abandoned me.

I was loved. I was cared for. I was provided for.

So many people (myself included for a very long time) think that just because I didn't have a bad childhood, it means that I shouldn't have had to deal with emotions of sadness, anger, loneliness or depression.

But I did, and I still do.

This is the first time that I can admit, as an adult, 'out loud' (in writing) that I struggle with depression. And not just the six years of postpartum depression that I am so open about. Fearful that I would end up in a mental health hospital like my mother. No, that depression is public knowledge. I've even written a bestselling book about it. I've publicly spoken about it. I continue to speak about it everywhere, and I've healed from it.

This depression is deeper it seems. This depression started when I was a little girl, and it continues to randomly haunt me.

I flashback again to that moment on New Year's Eve, standing on the water's edge. A blanket wrapped around my bare shoulders to shield me from the cool, brisk air. My bare feet planted firmly in the cold, wet sand, as if they were stuck in concrete. I couldn't move. I just stood there, the words *I want to die* running through my mind like a stock ticker. A tiny part of me is terrified that a moment will come when I might hear them again.

The thing is, I had a plan for my life. By thirty years old I was going to be married, with two kids, and have a successful career as an architect.

I had it all figured out.

I was going to have the career like my dad and be this amazing stay-at-home mom like my mother was. It's what I had always wanted. Amidst the unexplainable emotional sadness as a child, I at least knew what my life was going to look like as an adult.

I was doing "all the right things"—checking all the boxes.

I consistently had straight A's all through school.

I earned my Bachelors of Architecture degree.

I secured a really great job right out of college.

I breezed through my licensing exams in thirteen months.

I rose as high as I felt I could at the firm I was at, in a field that was primarily male-dominated, and then I started my own firm.

I had a wonderful business partner, and we had a successful business.

I bought a home—all on my own.

I was twenty-seven years old with the 'perfect' life. Everything was going according to my plan.

Everything…except a husband and kids.

Yeah, that part of the plan hadn't quite worked itself out yet. That part of the plan constantly reminded me of my loneliness, bringing up familiar thoughts and emotional sadness like those that plagued my childhood.

Once again, I found myself thinking, *I should be happy*. But I wasn't.

I eventually met my husband on a blind date when I was twenty-nine.

We both rode motorcycles (dirt bikes) and had mutual friends that insisted we know each other. Months, and dare I say years, of being the single friend tagging along to everyone else's wedding, I gave in and finally said, "Sure, give him my number."

We had two phone calls, and he seemed like a nice guy who shared a recreational interest in riding. A week or so later, butterflies in my stomach, I walked down my driveway, fully geared up in my motocross attire with my helmet in hand, to finally meet in person this guy I was *supposed* to know.

I had no idea what he looked like until he pulled up in his friend's truck, opened the door, and walked up the driveway to meet me. No pressure, right?

He's cute, I thought. *And damn, he's in his street clothes!*

I was embarrassed.

Should I have waited to change into my gear? Were we supposed to talk first? All kinds of thoughts flooded my brain as I awkwardly maneuvered our first meeting.

Our first date was fun, although not really ideal for getting to know someone. A lot of stopping at trail crossings giving thumbs up and head nods, but not a whole lot of conversation. It's pretty difficult to talk over the *braaap, braaap* of a four-stroke Honda ripping up the dirt ahead of you.

That was 2003, and in 2005 we got married after a quick three-month engagement. I was thirty-one—a little behind in my plan but feeling the peace and joy of finally having found my partner, of having love. It was the happiness that I needed, that I longed for, that up until that point was missing. Now my life was perfect, or so I thought.

Our marriage has had its share of ups and downs, as have most marriages. Marriage isn't easy. No relationship worth keeping and growing and deepening is ever easy. It's work, but I love my husband, and we keep working at it, together.

There are some days where I'm in awe of how he's stood by me. Periods in my life when I was not happy, not nice, not myself. The two most prominent periods were two that I have already alluded to: my mother's death and my postpartum depression.

Those are periods where one would expect a little sadness and loss. Those are periods where depression is a little easier to swallow because something happened to 'cause' it.

The thing about depression is that it is riddled with guilt and shame, but at least during those two times, I could blame it on 'something'.

I still struggle with depression some days. In fact, there are days where nothing happens to make me feel that certain way. It's not that I find myself in the grips of depression frequently anymore; however, there are still times when it sneaks up on me. No events or triggers.

There are some days when I wake up and can't shake myself out of certain thoughts or emotions—even though I know better, even though I know my mind is powerful. I just feel blah and foggy. I can't focus or think or make a decision. Some days I just want to cry.

"Mind over matter, mind over matter." I can say it a hundred times, but it won't erase the feelings.

There are days where, to the outside world and even to my husband, everything looks fine, everything looks good. But inside, it feels like the world is crumbling around me. And for no 'reason'.

I've got a great husband who loves me to the moon and back a million times. I've got two beautiful, handsome, smart young boys who love me to the moon and back a million times. I've got family and friends who support me no matter what and love me to the moon and back a million times.

I have love all around me. That is what keeps me going.

I can do all the work to take care of myself. I can practice my daily self-care, as preventative care, and in fact, that's what I help my clients do in their own lives. But some days, all the self-care in the world won't help.

There are still days where that just doesn't matter. There are days where I can't explain it, but the sadness and depression bubble up and attempt to take hold of my life. My perfectly great, happy, privileged life.

On New Year's Eve 2016-17, I stood at the water's edge, wanting to die. Crying up to Heaven, "God, please take me! Send me an angel and take me away."

I was pleading for the pain to go away. The pain of business failures. The pain of strained relationships. The pain of a disconnected marriage. There wasn't one thing, one event, one instance to cause my pain—it was the culmination of several years' worth of experiences. It just became too much.

I wanted to die.

Today I sit here and write this story, publicly, out loud sharing a little piece of my life with you.

I didn't have a bad childhood. My adulthood is one that most of the world's population would dream to experience even just a fraction of. My life isn't perfect, nor am I. I have challenges and struggles and unexplainable emotions and pain, just like the person behind me in the grocery store checkout line may, and I'd never even know.

I continue to rise above my pain. I continue to persevere through the tough days, the tough moments. The moments I would much rather crawl back into bed with the covers over my head, pulling completely away from life and reality. Oh, that would be so much easier.

However, I don't stay there. I rise above my circumstances—'normal' as they may be— and create new circumstances for myself.

People used to describe me as shy when I was a little girl. I'm not shy anymore, especially when it comes to following my passion and pursuing my dreams. Give me your ear, and I will spill it all, my story, my life. I'm not ashamed of my past. I'm not ashamed of where I've been, even when that's been to the deepest, darkest caverns of despair. My journey is what shapes me. It's what continues to pave the path I'm on.

I've mended the relationships with my dad and my sister. My husband and I are in a much better place. Things aren't perfect, but we are committed to work through our challenges and grow old together, as a family, with love.

Today, I get to help women stand up and put themselves first. Care for themselves on every level, so they can be the best version of themselves. I get to be the example for them, living in integrity of what I teach. Me first. You first. Not in a selfish way, but in a self-care way.

I thank God I didn't walk into the water that New Year's Eve. I thank God I took a step, but that step was backward. Not backward on my journey, but backward away from pain and hurt and fear. A step to rise above the pain and hurt and fear. A step towards my purpose on this planet.

Standing on the water's edge, I really, truly, honestly wanted to die.

I'm forty-four years old today, and I struggle with depression. I don't let that stop me. I recognize it now, and I know how to battle it. I take care of myself. I get honest with myself. I kick out guilt and put myself first, sometimes for extreme self-care when I need to but always out of love for my family and those around me. I am quick to turn to my community for guidance and support.

I cling onto the hope and faith that no matter how lonely, sad or hurt I may be feeling, for any good reason or not, I always have God.

Standing strong and powerful and more confident than ever, today I rise. Like the tide. Today the water lifts me, with my community around me.

Standing tall in Reno, NV, **I** rise.

Together, we rise.

This is Reno Rising.

Pamela Zimmer

Pamela Zimmer lives in Reno, NV with her husband, Will, and their two boys, Zackery and Brayden. After thirteen years as an architect, Pamela quit her career for motherhood. Postpartum depression and bankruptcy turned her life upside down but also showed her a new possibility. If you had said that someday she'd be a professional speaker, life coach, and bestselling author, she would have laughed.

Today that is exactly what she does, living life on her terms, embodying her work of self-care. She loves God, yoga, spa days with bubbly, and cozying up on the couch with a blanket, popcorn and a movie.

Pamela enjoys the outdoors, playing soccer with her boys, and writing, whether it be poetry, a blog post or working on one of her new book projects. She'll be the first to tell you, self-care isn't selfish, it's essential.

The Power of Powerlessness

By Dr. Erin Oksol

"Would you like to walk the entire red carpet, Dr. Erin?" the emcee asked after she called my name. "Oh yes I would," I exclaimed in front of the room of six-hundred guests who came to attend the awards luncheon. I had just kissed my adoring and proud husband, and as my heart beat with joy, gratitude, and excitement, I could hear my friends and colleagues cheering for me. After over eleven-thousand votes were cast, I had received the award of one of the top twenty most powerful women in Northern Nevada.

Walking across the room to the red carpet, memories flashed before me of what it took to come to this moment, and what the word "powerful" now came to mean to me. The irony was not lost on me that just over five short years before earning this award, I was the most powerless I had ever been in my life. Little did I know then, that through that powerlessness I would embark on my journey of regaining power in my life.

Powerlessness stared me in the face, looming over me as I woke up in jail. Yep. You read that right. This powerful, loved, smart woman spent twenty-eight days in jail. I didn't really wake up, so much as 'came to'. 'Waking up' is a euphemism us alcoholics like to use. Yep. You read that right too. This highly educated psychologist is a recovering alcoholic, and my best thinking landed me in jail. I know. I get paid to help people think better. Think healthier. Take care of themselves. Shouldn't I have known better? Shouldn't I have been able to save myself? Shouldn't I have been able to lean on the support and love of my husband, friends, and family and prevent the DUI that landed me in jail? Well, I sure thought so, too!

The day I woke up in jail, I realized the truth about myself. I was powerless over alcohol. I realized I had been imprisoned by something other than alcohol for years…perfectionism.

Let me tell you a little bit about my tumultuous love-hate relationship with perfectionism. It was the first 'ism' I ever struggled with. It was fueled by shame and fear—what I now refer to as the 'gateway drugs' to pain and suffering.

I knew since I was a young girl that I wanted to be a therapist. How can that be, you might ask? I have no idea. No explanation. But it was a gift not having to wander, trying to discover my calling, purpose or career path. I also knew that I wanted to grow up and be perfect. Yep. Perfect. Who wouldn't want to be perfect? I was on a mission.

I excelled in everything I attempted, and I had a 4.0 GPA all throughout my high school years and undergraduate career. I was pre-med, took the entrance exam to medical school, and was slated to apply to medical school. I was told growing up that a doctorate was the highest degree, the highest profession, and the most noble, so that's what I headed towards.

One of my last college courses was biochemistry, and we did not mix. I failed my first exam. I remember calling my parents, sobbing, with my first true failure experience, in shock that I failed. But I was in more shock when my father exclaimed, with a sordid satisfaction, "Congratulations!"

Excuse me? Did you hear me, Dad? I remember thinking, in shock. After restating the terrible news that I had failed, he lovingly replied, "It's about time you failed at something." He told me it was all going to be okay, and this failure experience was an important part of life. My perfectionism was having a field day! I was mad, frustrated, and ashamed.

It was my first encounter with the concept of feeling powerless. I could not pass these chemistry courses and remember asking my academic advisor, "Why do I have to learn all this chemistry? I just want to be a therapist and help people!" My advisor helped me realize that I wanted to be a psychologist, not a psychiatrist (I thought psychiatrists were psychologists and didn't realize the difference between the two).

I then thankfully redirected my educational path and applied to graduate school in clinical psychology and was accepted into my first-choice program. I sailed through the next seven years of higher education with more perfect grades and high accolades. My perfectionism and I were glued at the hip, happily intertwined, and I loved learning about the career I knew I always wanted to be a part of. I loved performing and proving my worth in academics, as it easily puffed up my sense of belonging, worthiness, and self-esteem.

After earning my doctorate, I spent the next several years specializing in treating children and adolescents. While I loved it and had a special way of connecting with young children and teenagers, I wanted to start my own family. So we did.

The first of our three children was born and life as a working mother was both exciting, complicated, and overwhelming to me. Child psychologists often have to see their clients after school and in the evenings. I was helping other children and families get well, and meanwhile, my own mental health was deteriorating, and I was rarely spending time with my own family.

Since perfectionism is fueled by having an excessive need for control, becoming a mother triggered intense anxiety in me. I felt extremely out of control and powerless over this tiny little human being and felt ill-equipped at being a successful working mother.

A low-grade depression ensued, and over the course of the next year, turned into a full-grade clinical depression.

My perfectionism was in full force. It dictated everything in my life. I rarely took risks in my professional or personal life. I became socially anxious and tried to fill the hole in my soul with outside things like clothes, fancy cars, a nice house, and approval from others. I went from being the happy, successful, top-of-her-class superstar, to a clinically depressed, financially stressed, hopeless, despondent, and anxious woman.

I soon reached the pinnacle of my powerlessness, what I call my 'emotional rock bottom'. I became extremely ashamed of my mental state. I had a supportive and loving husband, two gorgeous children, and on the outside, a perfect, beautiful life. Healers often cannot heal themselves and being unaware of how severe my own depression was, I concluded I was simply ungrateful and unworthy and began to turn on myself even more. I was imprisoned by shame. I was shackled by feelings of unworthiness and was disgusted by myself.

After giving birth to our second child, Emily, I experienced debilitating post-partum depression. I decided to take a week-long vacation with her and returned home to Minnesota so that my family could give me some much-needed rest. I was doing whatever I could to escape my depression, but nothing was working. I was convinced I would never be happy again. That week, one of my family members poured me a vodka cranberry. I had never drunk hard alcohol other than an occasional margarita on girl's night out. I remember the effect being powerful and immediate. I experienced a relief from and a numbing of my depression. I remember feeling happy for the first time in a long time. I continued to anesthetize my depression that week with more vodka cranberry cocktails. I returned home to Reno with this newfound coping mechanism for my overwhelming life. Within one year I was a daily drinker. Alcohol worked—until it didn't work anymore. My disease progressed quickly and ferociously. I drank alone, and nobody knew the secrets I was hiding.

Over the next several years I attempted to get sober, and when I would relapse, I attempted to admit myself to inpatient programs. I answered the questions they asked honestly and would check a 'yes' on all of the assessment questions. However, when it came time to admit me, I was always denied because I had a loving husband and/or a home to return to. I was a 'functional alcoholic', some might say, and continued to have a successful career. Therapist after therapist would hear my story, but they always seemed to want to discuss the root causes of my drinking instead of the drinking itself. I, in turn, always concluded that I was not a real alcoholic. Because of this assumption, every failed attempt to quit fed my belief that I was bad, selfish, ungrateful, and unworthy. I had no idea I was sick needing to get well. I thought I was bad needing to 'get good'. My shame increased to toxic proportions.

We were surprised to learn we were pregnant with our third child. While we were elated, my husband and I were terrified. I was struggling with intermittent depression and relapsing in my alcoholism. When Zachary was six months old, I was arrested for a DUI and landed in jail. How could this happen to me? I was a doctor. I had a loving husband. I had three beautiful children and a successful psychology practice. Friends and family who loved me. How did I get to that point?

For the first nine days in jail, my husband Garth did not speak to me. I didn't know if he was going to leave me or let me fight for my life, sobriety, and family one last time. In those nine days, I experienced true powerlessness. I decided in those days to turn my life and my will over to the care of my higher power—God. I admitted to my innermost self that I was powerless over alcohol. I remember waking up the morning after I surrendered to freshly fallen snow. I heard God whisper to me, "Erin, you are white as snow." On the ninth day, Garth called me on the web-based visiting system. He said the words my heart was dying to hear. "I'm going to give you a chance to get well." I knew it was my chance to heal. I didn't know how, but I knew I was given an opportunity to finally break free from my prison of shame and recover from my disease of alcoholism.

After twenty-eight days in jail, I entered a thirty-day inpatient program for substance abuse. I learned the true root cause of my disease-shame and perfectionism. Slowly, piece by piece, I laid a new foundation for myself. This foundation included self-acceptance, tools for living life on life's terms, and learning how to show up and feel my feelings—all of them. The good, the bad, and the ugly.

I finally felt like I had joined the human race! I didn't feel apart from, or different, for the first time, and I loved it. There was no more room for comparing, shaming myself, or self-destruction. Fear and anger were replaced with peace, forgiveness, self-reflection, and self-compassion. I cleaned up my diet, went to the gym, dove head first into personal development, and started to rise from the ashes. I beat my depression, anxiety, and perfectionism.

I got real with people for the first time. I showed them the 'underbelly', so to speak, of my heart, sharing vulnerably what I really thought, wanted, feared, and hoped for. It was intoxicating, in the best way. Being my real, authentic self was impossible while being perfect—so one of them had to go. I broke up with my perfectionism. I fell in love with fumbling forward, stepping outside of my comfort zone, and trying new things. It was the first time in my life where I experienced some real, authentic power.

My quiet, anxious, and reserved self morphed into an exuberant, happy, bubbly person who loved connecting—truly connecting with people. I started to collect friends like seashells. Choosing the best of the best. The brightest, shiniest, happiest, most loving, honest, and kind people I could find. In turn, I became attractive to others. They wanted to be around my light, my energy, and my joy. Through learning how to stop trying to please everyone, I started forming deep, meaningful relationships.

Due to the fact that I was developing a growth mindset, I started my own business. For five years, I was in a network marketing company that I was deeply committed to. I learned much about leadership, personal development, and how to be a savvy business woman. At first, I was thriving. I was asked to train on the big stage and realized I loved speaking and leading! I loved sharing my expertise in psychology and applying it to business - helping women become successful and financially free!

However, shame and powerlessness lurked right around the corner, waiting to prey on me again. For some unknown reason, I could not successfully enroll others in my business. My leaders could not explain it, and I was told things like:

"Don't be so professional."
"Maybe you're dressed too nice and it's not approachable."
"You're not duplicatable."
"The only way to fail is to quit."

I felt confused, stuck, and the shame and self-doubt starting to gain power again.

I decided to hire a business coach and a mindset coach. I learned about the world of coaching for the first time. I fell in love with the industry and started voraciously studying it, watching and learning from those who were paving the way. I realized they had what I wanted. Time freedom. Successful clients. Higher pay. Autonomy and a greater impact.

A dream was birthed in me. A small seed that has now grown into the largest of oak trees. I wanted to be a coach and I wanted to be a speaker.

My business was birthed at a local public swimming pool. Yep, you read that right. Lying in the sun on the fourth of July weekend, I started a conversation with the woman next to me. Watching our children play in the pool, we got to know one another. She was a marketing genius. I honored the nudge to tell her, a perfect stranger, my dream of being a coach and speaker. I told her with my background in psychology, I believed I could help people create meaningful change in their lives and businesses. That I could serve so many more than I could seeing clients on an individual basis in my therapy office. However, I felt somewhat powerless again. I had no knowledge in how to build a successful business, how to effectively market myself, and had no sales experience. But I knew my power often came when I felt powerless. I would ask for help—a lot of it.

I followed her lead and created my website, brand, and marketing plan. I became influential on social media and my visibility grew, one step at a time. My network marketing company became intrusive and overbearing and asked me to choose between staying in their company or growing my own. I chose to pursue my dream, with no guarantee of success. I was shunned by many of the women in that company whom I believed would be my lifelong friends. I grieved the loss like a death. I felt like I was out on the skinny branches of the tree, dangling in uncertainty.

But I went for it. All in. I told my marketing guru I wanted to be a professional speaker. I admitted to her that I had no idea how one does that, to which she replied, "I think you speak." We chuckled and filled my calendar with speaking engagements. I got in front of my ideal clients—anyone who would listen. I spoke forty-three times in the first year. I enrolled individual coaching clients and they started to see real change - fast. They started to sing my praises and my coaching business was born.

I now lead my own one-day workshops where I host hundreds of people who come to change their lives. They come to grow their belief in themselves and chase their dreams. I help them make their vision a reality, all with fun, humor, and grace. I am growing a tribe of women who have each other's backs. Women who take a stand against perfectionism and people pleasing. Women who honor each other's bravery and who applaud each other's vulnerability.

The power of powerlessness. Honoring the nudge. Listening to that voice within you that knows what you want and then taking the steps to go after it. Taking fear along the ride with you. This seems to be where the magic happens. Where life gets really good.

I want this for you. I want this for all of us. The next time life takes you down a path you had not expected, and perhaps you feel powerless, perhaps it is the right and perfect pivot that will direct you to your right and perfect path.

While this path has not been perfect, it's mine. I own the scrapes and bruises and wrong turns. I own the victories and celebrations and successes. In the process, I have broken the cycle of being addicted to perfection. My children and I ask each other the same three questions every night, as they are now my measure of a truly successful life:

1) How was I brave today?

2) How did I fumble forward today?

3) How was I kind?

Train your brain for true success. Remind it to take risks and be courageous, and never forget the power of being powerless. For in those moments we are most likely to be authentic, vulnerable, and open to receive. In that openness, we can easily connect with others and our true selves.

Who knew that through surrendering one can actually win the battle? Who knew that being vulnerable could feel so powerful!

Dr. Erin Oksol

Dr. Erin Oksol is a high performance and mindset strategist, psychologist, corporate trainer, professional speaker, online social marketer, and bestselling author. She is the founder of Massive Business Success Coaching and has a small private psychology practice in Reno. Her mission is helping business owners/entrepreneurs turn their passions into profits, creating a massive impact by doing what they love.

With fifteen years of clinical experience counseling and coaching clients, she brings her expertise in human behavior and change to help others go from where they are to where they want to be, so they can create a business and life they are obsessed with!

She is married to Garth and has three children—Grace (sixteen), Emily (thirteen), and Zachary (seven).

Kidnapped

By Alexanne Stone

I feel like a fraud. I just had the honor of spending the evening with some of the women who've written their stories for this Reno Rising book, and I feel like a fraud. Theirs are stories of courage, bravery, pain, abuse, loss, death, rape depression, and every single woman has risen out of her pain. They have taken life on in a way that has moved and inspired me deeply and profoundly in this moment. I feel like my whole life has changed simply by spending the evening with these amazing women, listening to their stories.

My original story is a fraud, a *skimming* over the topic of life. One where I touch something and then, like the stove being too hot, I jump away only to cover the story with some fake attempt to pretend that the things that happened to me never happened, and that I am absolutely healed with everything now in the past. It's a lie. I decided it was time for a do-over.

My past started at the bottom of the staircase. I remember the moment as if it were yesterday. I was sitting at the bottom of the long, winding staircase that led up to my parents' bedroom, looking out the window at the apple orchard. It must have been spring because the trees were bursting in flowers – a beautiful cloud of pink. I was sitting with my chin in my hand, elbow on my knee, contemplating life. I remember thinking that no one understood me, least of all my mother. It was at that moment that I asked God to make sure that I understood other people and their pain. That, when I was a grown-up, I could understand any person who sat across from me, letting them know that someone else understood what they'd been through. That I understood their pain. I was five years old.

You know how they say, "be careful what you wish for"?

I'd missed the bus one evening, somewhere near 24th and Wilshire Boulevard in Santa Monica. I was supposed to go to a meeting that night, and I still have no idea why I didn't just drive. But I'd missed the bus.

It was dusk, and the meeting was supposed to start at seven. I was standing in an alcove in a dimly lit storefront. I remember the windows on either side of me as I was waiting for the bus, standing right in front of the store door. The store was closed.

In 1978, 24th and Wilshire was not the bustling street it is now. There were no restaurants, galleries, or wall-to-wall businesses. The alcove where I was standing was in front of a car wash—a big empty concrete lot with a closed carwash on one end and nothing else nearby. It was getting dimmer outside, and there was still no bus.

A man approached and leaned against one of the alcove windows. I remember sizing him up. Over six feet, very husky, a big man with reddish hair and pale skin. He just stared at me. I tried to ignore him, but he walked up to me, bent over my face, and looked me in the eyes.

"You didn't realize it when you woke up this morning, but your number is up today!"

I felt my heart leap into my throat as I gasped, looking into his cold, green eyes. If you can imagine, I was so naïve that I wasn't sure what that meant, but I had the feeling it wasn't good. Everything that happened next was a blur. He dragged me into the empty car wash lot and threw me down on the concrete. I remember the concrete, still warm from the sun's heat, and the stones digging into my skin as I fell.

He began to open my purse and go through my belongings. I felt like I was separate from what was happening, and that my body wasn't attached to my brain. Everything was happening in slow motion—time had suddenly stopped moving at normal speed and had slowed down to a crawl. Even his words as he spoke to me seemed to come from a tape recorder set on the slowest speed. I was having a hard time understanding what he was saying as he was asking me my name and where I lived; pulling the things out of my purse, examining them, and again asking me who I was.

There were two important things that were in my mind at this moment in time. The first was that I'd just had a hysterectomy at age twenty-five. I still had the stitches in my lower belly, and I was terrified that he would rip those stitches open and I would bleed out on the street.

I'd been hospitalized once, and the old man across the hall from me had wanted to die. No one would let him go. He'd tried ripping out the tubes, and when he did, the machines notified the staff what he'd done. So, they plugged him in again, keeping him alive. He would beckon me from his bed to come over and pull the tubes out for him. He had an emergency, and they rushed him to heart surgery. Once he was back in his room, after the surgery, he ripped open his stitches and bled out.

The memory of the old man stuck in my mind and, at that moment, on that concrete, at that isolated car wash, I was terrified that my fate would be similar.

The other thing that came to mind was a speaker I'd gone to see. I cannot remember his name. At that time in the 1970's the police were advocating that if you were facing rape, you should scream for your life at the top of your lungs. Alone...in a car wash? On the dirty concrete with a man over 6 feet tall who was three times heavier? A man who just told me my number was up? I didn't think so!

The guy who'd done the lectures said that if you were facing danger, do one of three things. If it was inevitable that you were going to be raped and live, just lay down and take the rape and get help for it after. If you were going to be killed, make sure you killed first. The third suggestion was that if it was possible to make friends with the rapist, make friends. The speaker had this theory that sometimes rapists are just lonely people looking for comfort. His complete theory—*do whatever it takes to survive!*

Regardless of your opinion on hearing this advice, I had taken it to heart at that time, and I opted for survival. Survival at any cost! I began a conversation with this man while lying on the concrete, in the summer heat, in Santa Monica, alone, at a deserted car wash.

I remember starting to ask him how his day was. What kind of work did he do? He was dressed in green coveralls, and I knew he was a mechanic of some kind. I told him that we didn't meet by accident. I told him that God had put us together to know each other. *Nothing* happened by accident and that we were supposed to know one another. The more I talked, the more he listened.

The more I listened, the more he talked. He told me about his horrible childhood and how life had been so hard for him. In Los Angeles there were so many people with money and cars and big houses, and all he had was a crummy apartment and a mechanics job that didn't pay anything. He said life was so hard, and he was just done with all of it.

I could feel the hairs on the back of my neck stand up as I continued to talk to him. My skin felt like it was on fire. Every cell in my body was on alert, and I was listening to him in a way I'd never listened to anyone before. I knew with every breath that my last one could be next, so I focused on everything about him that there was to see. I focused on his every word.

He continued to go through all my things, turning my purse over and dumping my treasures on the concrete. He took my driver's license and put it in his back pocket memorizing my name while he did. He said he was just so lonely and just wanted to be loved. He started pouring out his life story to me—abusive father, rough childhood, trouble with alcohol and drugs as an adult. He said he had nowhere else to turn and was ready to just give up. He said he didn't want to give up alone but wanted to take someone with him when he went.

I took his every word into my heart and weighed my every move gauging it for survival.

At one point in time, he was lying on the concrete with his head in my lap crying. I was petting his head and soothing his tears with my fingers on his face as he told me how unloved he had been his whole life. He said he wanted someone beautiful like Marilyn Monroe and knew that he could never get that kind of woman. I kept reassuring him, telling him that everything would be all right, that God was right here with us, comforting us. I started helping him see his future and how he could find love if he would just give it more time.

He said he needed a girlfriend to go on living. He asked me if I would be his girlfriend.

I remember my response at that moment. Every skill I'd ever honed toward survival kicked in. I acted like it was the best idea I'd ever heard. The words, "Yes…I'll be your girlfriend" gushed out of my mouth while I swallowed the bile rising in my throat. He laid in my lap and actually fell asleep. Terrified, I let him lay without moving a muscle until he awoke again a few minutes later.

He bolted upright and grinned. "I have a great idea," he exclaimed. "Let's go on our first date!"

Pulling me up by the wrist, he said, "There's an ice cream shop down the street. Let's take the bus down there. Let me take you for ice cream." I knew this was my chance to get away.

Back to the alcove we went, and when he saw the bus coming, he pulled me close to him. Looking into my eyes, he said, "If you say anything about this to anyone, I'll kill you!"

We got on the bus. He shoved me into a window seat and crowded me as he sat next to me. I tried to look around, but he was focused on me with a glare that froze the blood in my veins. When it was time to get off the bus, he grabbed my hand and pulled me to him. I knew that he was preventing me from doing anything to protect myself. It looked to those around us like we were lovers.

We got a table at an almost empty restaurant and ordered ice cream from a teenaged waitress with blonde hair. I will always remember her chirpy, friendly, *here to serve you* voice.

Choking down the ice cream sundae he chose for me, I said I had to go to the bathroom. "I'll walk you there," he said. We walked to the back of the store to the ladies' room, and as we walked, I hatched a plan. I could write a message in lipstick on the mirror.

When we got to the door, he pulled me close, leaned down, and whispered into my ear, "When you come out, we'll go back in together. If I find anything written anywhere, I mean *anything… anywhere*, I *will* kill you!"

I knew it was too risky to leave anything on the mirror. I thought maybe I could write something on the toilet paper, but at the last moment decided it was too hazardous an idea. Good thing. True to his word, he followed me back into the bathroom where he actually unrolled the toilet paper to look for a message. I let out my breath as we began walking back into the restaurant's main room.

We moved to the cash register to pay the bill. I was standing behind his left shoulder while he paid. I remember this vividly because the chirpy, friendly waitress was asking how everything was. While he was telling her that it was fine, I was standing behind him cautiously shaking my head from side to side and silently mouthing "Help!", over and over again, while watching him to see if he knew what I was doing. She just smiled, rang up the order, and handed him his change.

When we left the ice cream shop, he decided it was a beautiful night and that we should walk back to my house on 24th. I remember the feel of his hand holding mine as we walked, big...rough...hard. It took every ounce of strength inside me to surrender to this moment. Acting like I was his girlfriend would keep me alive. We talked the whole way back about him and his life again, and he said he was so happy that he was going to have me as a girlfriend because I was so sweet and so easy to get along with. Of course I was. I was determined to live!

As we rounded the corner to 24th, I realized that if he came into my home, it would be the end. I just couldn't stop imagining that he would see my stitches, rip them open and I would die. Or he would rape me, and I would be damaged inside. Or he would hurt my other roommates somehow. I had to do whatever I could to keep him out of the house.

I told him that I still needed to go to my meeting. Even though I'd missed the original bus, the meeting was still going on, and I wanted to go. I asked him, "Would you walk me to my car?" He agreed.

As we were walking up the incline on the sidewalk, he stopped under a streetlight, faced me, looked me in the eyes and declared, "I still want to fuck you though." Again, I felt fear wash over my entire body. My knees got rubbery, and it was difficult to breathe. I put a light smile on my face, stepped in closer to him suggestively, and said, "Oh, I want you to! But we're boyfriend and girlfriend now, and I'd like to get to know you a little better before we do it for the first time. Would that be okay with you?"

Silence. Then he slowly said, "I'd at least like a kiss." I don't know where I got my courage, but I replied, "Okay, but only on the cheek for now." To my absolute surprise, he agreed. With my hand in his, I turned and started toward the car again.

I pulled the keys out of my purse and walked across the street to the driver's door. At that moment, I begged, "Please God…please let me just get into my car and drive away. Please don't let him hurt me and *please* don't let him get into the car!"

As I opened the door, I remember that my hands were shaking, and I was sweating. I remember that I was so afraid that my lip was twitching. He leaned over to kiss me, and I turned my left cheek toward him to receive it. He kissed my cheek as I got into my car, put the keys into the ignition, turned on the engine and drove away.

I survived! I'm alive!

He called me the next morning. I packed up my belongings and moved away.

I had nightmares for ten years. Lucid dreams. A man standing over me with a knife—always faceless—there every night. Was it him? Was I creating something in the future? What was happening to me? I lost a lot of weight and couldn't sleep through a whole night.

I became afraid of everyone and everything. I stored weapons in every room in the house—scissors in the shower, a baseball bat by the front door, a knife in my sock, knives in my car, a tire iron under the driver's seat. Always afraid that he would return or that someone like him would find me and the next time wouldn't end so well. I watched everyone in a crowd, listened for footsteps behind me, locked the car doors as soon as I got in, and kept my keys in my hands to unlock my front door rather than reaching for them in my purse. I jumped at every noise in my house hearing it as loud and threatening.

A friend suggested I visit a hypnotherapist. In the hypnotherapy session, I uncovered the details of this memory and thought it was resolved. I still had the nightmares. The hypnotherapist suggested I visit a Neuro-Linguistic Programming (NLP) practitioner. I had no idea what that was, but desperately wanted out of the victim life I'd been living.

NLP was like lifting a veil off my life. Lifting the cloud. It's hard to explain what NLP is. The easiest way I can describe what NLP does, is it involves the way we make and store our memories—in pictures, sounds and feelings—which gives us a new set of tools to make absolutely profound changes in our lives easily and quickly, simply by changing those pictures, sounds and feelings.

The first three-hour session was intense and revealing, and I began to understand how I was recreating this victim consciousness every single day. Reliving this and other scathing memories, I remember being in tears and writhing in pain for fear of losing my life. Not only from this memory, but from others where I'd faced death at gunpoint, knifepoint, been smothered, choked, and raped. I began to understand how I had recreated the fear of these events happening over and over again, every single day. I finally understood that I had been doing all of this in my imagination! It was time to shift my life.

And shift it, I did! I did another NLP session the next day—equally intense and equally revealing. I let go of so much of the pain that I had stored, and I got a new outlook on life. I determined that I needed to know how to do this for other people and help them transform their lives.

I decided to become certified as an NLP practitioner myself. By the time I turned thirty-nine, I had completed the training all the way through master practitioner level and was in the final training to become a certified NLP trainer. What I wished for at age five became my reality as I worked with people to help them understand their pain and transform their lives.

Someone once said that "victim" is only a label we wear; we just don't know we don't have to wear it. To me, it goes so much deeper than that. The vibration the word "victim" creates every time we think or speak it out loud perpetuates the label, the feeling, and even the manifestation. As we grow in our lives, we get the opportunity to not only let go of the label, but to create a vision that is exciting and empowering. We create a life that manifests the way that we truly are. This is what NLP has done for me.

Writing this story has been confronting to say the least. Almost agonizing to really share as I have had to reveal myself in memories that I believed I'd buried over the years. Are those memories buried or do they give me the strength to be who I am today? Or do they still come up whenever I have a moment of quiet, a moment of reflection, or a moment like tonight—one where women share the absolute *rawness* of being alive and how they've conquered their pasts.

Even though my two-and-a-half-hour ordeal was over, and I have, through NLP, been able to release the emotional impact, this is the kind of memory you never forget. I got what I'd wished for when I was just five years old, that whenever someone sits across from me in their pain, I would be able to empathize deeply and guide them to reclaim their power and their lives. It is what I did for him—and it saved my life!

Alexanne Stone

Alexanne started her career in Silicon Valley selling Apple computers. In the midst of her early sales career, she was introduced to Neuro-Linguistic Programming and established the San Jose School of NLP and Hypnotherapy.

Finishing up her sales career in Santa Clara, Alexanne moved to Grand Rapids, Michigan to be near family. Here, Alexanne was the non-profit director of a medical professional emergency response training organization under the Office of the Surgeon General and Homeland Security for the following five years.

Missing the west coast weather, Alexanne decided to connect with friends in the Reno area and has enjoyed living there since 2011. After leaving the corporate world, and newly married, she and her husband, Tim, have chosen to focus on expanding NLP through creating new programs soon to go nationwide.

A decorated Vietnam-era U.S. Air Force Veteran, Alexanne is also an accomplished artist. Her work includes oils, watercolor, colored pencil, charcoal, pen and ink, and moulage.

Weathering the Storm

By Jamie Ward

Have you ever been in hell? Let me tell you what it feels like.

Your spirit has left your body. You are one of the walking dead. Demons with unrelenting souls surround you and they are all screaming, *welcome to hell. You are fucked.*

You are empty and helpless because your home is gone, and you cannot get it back. You feel lost when you yearn to be in your own bed and then suddenly realize you no longer have one. You are in fear because you don't know what to do. You are filled with guilt and anguish because you made a choice between life and death. You feel entirely alone in a nightmare and must defend yourself. You are destitute because you no longer have what comforts you. You are grieving and want to cry, but you can't. Disorder and confusion have taken over your mind. You are lost in a darkened maze of chaos with no end in sight. The demons have turned you into an empty shell and your mind into a fog of grey shadows.

My life as I once knew it was obliterated by the worst natural disaster in history. My hell was Hurricane Katrina and its aftermath. On August 29, 2005, the eye of the storm made landfall in Bay Saint Louis, Mississippi, where I lived with my husband, three-month-old daughter Renee, and four cats. The events that followed changed my life in unimaginable ways.

No, we didn't stay. We were invited by a friend in central Louisiana to weather the storm at his house. So, the day before the hurricane, our house was boarded up, our Jeep was packed and ready to go. It takes time to batten down the hatches, as it were, to secure your home, bring inside all your outside things, and decide what to take with you. *What should I take? What do I leave behind?* These words will haunt me for years.

I packed a pair of sweatpants and a couple of tops. We planned to be home in three days. I took only what the baby needed to get by on, which was a lot for a three-month-old.

Our friend didn't appreciate having our four cats at his house. We found that out during a hurricane evacuation the year before when he made our stay awkward and eventually unbearable. He constantly bitched about the cats and spritzed Lysol room spray, which was his hint that the cats were a nuisance; this time around, we didn't feel comfortable bringing all of them. We needed to keep the peace, so we had to make a choice. *Which cats do we take? Which cats stay behind?*

We decided to take Boo and Rudy. They were our inside cats. Socks and Lily would stay behind. They were strays, although they quickly became a part of the family when they set up residence outside our home. They knew how to fend for themselves. I put plenty of food and water under the house. They can weather the storm there and stay safe and dry. *They will be fine.* I had to convince myself of that.

We arrived at the friend's house by noon. He had not only his room spray but also a giant round air filtration machine for the living room. *What the hell? Like I'm going to let the cats turd on his floor and stink up the house?* His behavior was insulting. It has been said that guests, like fish, begin to smell after three days. Well, so do hosts.

Katrina hit the following morning. We learned that a thirty-five-foot storm surge was rushing through Bay Saint Louis. It took me a moment to mentally process it. Then I remembered the cats.

Socks and Lily! Oh, my God! They're dead!

My heart dropped into my stomach. Anguish and guilt took over me because I played Russian Roulette with their lives. They needed me, and I abandoned them. *Please, dear God, forgive me.* I envisioned what their nightmare must have been like: Swept away with the rushing tide, panicked and scrambling to the top for air, tumbling and turning beneath the water, slamming against debris that was washing away with them.

I had to put those thoughts in the back of my mind. The pain and regret were too much to bear, besides there was nothing I could do. I had to forget about them. Experiential avoidance quickly became my coping strategy and would continue for many years to come.

Then anger set in. We appreciated having a place to stay, but if we had felt welcomed to bring all four cats, Socks and Lily would be safe with us. *It's his fault. That fucker.*

We watched the crisis live on TV, flipping from one news station to another. *What happened to Bay Saint Louis?* There was a constant stream of news about the levee break in New Orleans, but nothing about the adjoining Mississippi Gulf Coast. The media forgot about our town that was actually hit with the eye of the storm. *What's the damage to The Gulf Coast?* We needed to know. Those of us who suffered our losses in Bay Saint Louis, Mississippi, felt short-changed by the TV coverage.

It had taken two days for a northern Mississippi news station to cover the destruction along The Coast. A helicopter hovered low along the shoreline. I could see the remnants of the hurricane's powerful winds and the strength of its water. Every home, every building was gone. Empty concrete foundations remained where there once were buildings. The leaves on the trees were as bare as a midwinter's day. The Gulf Coast was brown and lifeless. All streets that led north to south and east to west were covered with debris of the structures that lined them.

Which town are they flying over? I held onto hope that our home was still standing. It didn't look good. Everything was gone. There was only rubble of a crushed shoreline of communities. The Gulf Coast looked as though an atomic bomb had exploded in the sky above it.

Then I see it. *Oh my God!* The only landmark that remained standing among miles and miles of debris was the black and white steeple of Christ Episcopal Church across the street from our home. It was the needle in the haystack. A beacon from God that said, *I'm still here, but your home is not.*

How do you remain strong when everything that meant something is no longer there? I was numb and unable to process just how grim our situation has become.

When I was in college, I suffered the sudden loss of my boyfriend. A friend had given me a tiny bottle with a note on yellow paper rolled tightly inside it. I kept it in my jewelry box for twenty-six years. *I saw you on campus today, and you looked incredibly down. I'm thinking of you.* Whenever I needed a friend, I would open it, unravel the tiny piece of paper and remember that someone cared about me. It's strange how that is one of the first things I thought about that day. I wish I had that bottle.

My husband and I spent two weeks taking care of Katrina business and registered with both FEMA and The Red Cross for assistance. We made the three-hour drive back to Bay Saint Louis to see the damage for ourselves. The devastation was complete. There were no landmarks to indicate where we were. *Oh, there's the pink house. We're three blocks from home.* No, that landmark was gone. Each street looked the same. All homes were reduced to splintered wooden planks spread around the town like pixie sticks. People's belongings littered the landscape. Shirts and ties, sheets and towels, and white plastic shopping bags hung from trees like lace on an open window. I saw a tightly twisted red shirt entangled within a crushed chain-link fence and was aghast at the force of the wind and water that created this damage. I could smell death in the air.

Our home was reduced to a pile of broken wooden planks. The aluminum roof was torn apart like a sheet of paper. The concrete steps that led to the front porch were the only sound structure. *You can rebuild by starting from here.*

I called out for Socks and Lily, but my voice cracked into sobs. I found myself crying and screaming at the same time. The pain poured out of me. I was completely lost and helpless. I felt insignificant among the mountains of tattered ruins in our neighborhood. All was quiet. No people. Few cars. Not one bird chirped. I was anguished and deadened to my reality.

We put up an American flag in front of the concrete steps as a signal to others: *We were here.*

At the end of two weeks, there was nothing more for us to do. I had worn out my welcome with Mister Room Spray, and we needed to be with family who could help guide us.

It was time for the three of us to move on to my parents' home in Philadelphia, where I grew up. It was there I would plan our next steps. Before we left, I received a phone call from my brother. John and his family lived in Reno and owned a rental property that had just become available.

"Come to Reno, so you guys can regroup and decide what you are going to do."

"Thanks. No, we can't come to Reno. We'll be fine."

"Jamie, you have a new baby," he said. "You can either live in a FEMA trailer in a disaster area or you can come out here and live in a nice house."

This conversation went in circles. I could hear the dire tone in my brother's voice. *How bad can it be? We don't need to go to Reno.*

"Where are you going to live? You have nothing," he said.

John was insistent. I was in denial, despite seeing the destruction in person. My mind had shut down to my new reality of being homeless and unemployed, and I couldn't make one rational decision on my own. I was a robot going through the motions and living minute by minute.

Okay. We are going to Reno. My brother decided for me. End of story.

We dropped off Boo and Rudy at my brother-in-law's house, which is just outside of New Orleans, before our flight to Philadelphia. In hindsight, I don't know why we didn't take the cats with us, other than we weren't thinking straight. Once we were settled in Reno, we will fly back to New Orleans to get them.

I wanted to have Renee baptized while in Philadelphia. I didn't know when my immediate family would all be together again. Nothing fancy. Maybe dinner afterward. I had only two changes of clothes and needed something to get me through the next week or so, and I needed a church outfit for the baptism. I had to go shopping.

I took the escalator up to the ladies' department and looked all around me. I saw what seemed like miles of circular racks jammed with women's clothing. There was no order. It made no sense. It was clothing chaos. Demons were now screaming in my head. *What do I buy first? I need everything. Underwear? Jeans? Shoes? Someone tell me what to do!* I had to build a wardrobe from the ground up. The room moved in circles. I thought I was going to be sick or pass out. I had to get out of there. I was suffocating.

I drove to the mall twice in two days, panicked, and left empty-handed. On the third day, I focused on only what I needed for the baptism. A white dress for the baby, and a skirt and blouse for me, plus a pair of heels. *Done. I have to get out of here.*

My husband and I had been at each other's throats for weeks. We weren't a team in this catastrophe. We were all for one, at this point. The gauntlet was thrown. There was no taking back anything we said to one another. I was beginning to feel abandoned by his anger and the ongoing fights.

The demons came between us, and now we were enemies. I needed his shoulder to cry to on, but I was alone in my grief.

On the morning of the baptism, I didn't think it could be possible that, yet, another crisis would take me down and render me into shock and fear, but when you're in hell, it has no end.

My husband and I were still in fight mode, and as he always said, "I don't get angry, I get even." He wanted to hurt me, so he told me that he received a call from his sister the day before, when I was shopping for the baptism stuff. Boo and Rudy had escaped through an open door. They've been missing for 24 hours. "So there," he said. It was a deliberate sucker punch into my gut. Panic. Fear. I was completely freaked out. I was pissed off. I was scared. I felt as though my entire life rested on finding my cats. And it did. They were all that remained from my prior life—pre-Katrina. *We must find them. Dear God, will this nightmare ever end?*

No, it won't.

I was to stay in hell. The demons weren't done fucking with me.

Needless to say, the baptism was somber. It felt more like a funeral rather than the Holy sacrament of accepting Christ. Despite my internal pain and loathing for my husband, I felt safe, surrounded by the love and protection of my family.

The next morning, he flew back to New Orleans to search for the cats. It took him more than a week to find both Boo and Rudy, and I was able to breathe again. Everything will be okay now. I was eager to get to Reno.

Renee and I arrived in Reno late at night with only a duffle bag of stuff. I was emotionally drained but happy to be alone in a place that was my own. The next morning, I was flying back to New Orleans to help my husband bring Boo and Rudy out to Reno, so my brother and his wife took Renee while I was gone.

My first night in my new home was peaceful. There was no chaos. I was able to relax for the first time in five weeks. I had a calming sensation, the kind you get when you sip a glass of wine, and its warmth fills your entire body.

The next day, I arrived in New Orleans in the early evening. I was so happy to see Boo and Rudy and, by the way they had greeted me, they were happy too. They'd had their own hell. My husband and I settled into bed. Our flight to Reno was at 7 a.m.

I took a sleeping pill, picked up my little Ru-Ru and put him in bed between us. Suddenly, he gave a little twitch. I gently stroked his fur. *It's okay.* He jumped from the bed and hid in the open closet. I brought him back to bed with us, but his twitches became full-blown seizures. I bolted upright. I didn't know what was happening to him. The seizures came more frequently. I was freaking the fuck out. *I DO NOT KNOW WHAT TO DO.* We had to leave for Reno in a few hours. *We have to get him to a vet!* It was midnight. *Jesus Christ! Wake me from this hell hole!*

We rushed Rudy to the only open animal hospital. My adrenaline took over, and I felt no effects of the sleeping pill. I was wide fucking awake and exhausted at the same time. The animal hospital was operating on generators. It was chaos. It seemed that everyone had an emergency. We waited for four hours to see the vet who told us she didn't know what's wrong. Rudy continued to seize. *But, we are leaving for Reno in a couple of hours!* No, we cannot take him with us. It's too risky. *Okay. We'll come back when he's better.* So, without even saying goodbye to him, we left New Orleans with only Boo.

We called the vet immediately once we arrived at our house in Reno. My husband was standing beside me. The vet could not stop Rudy's seizures. She had been waiting to hear from us because the only thing to do was to put him down. He was suffering.

My heart pounded out of my chest. *This cannot be happening.* I looked at my husband. His eyes and face were already red. He gave me a nod, and with that, we both agreed that our little Rudy should be put to sleep.

This had to be my darkest hour. The pain was crushing and unbearable. Katrina had taken my little Rudy too. We held each other tightly and together we sobbed out loud and uncontrollably.

I cried until I had no more tears, only pain. I cried for him. I cried for all our losses. I had never experienced such intense stress and sustained grief as I had during those five weeks. Rudy's death was the end of it all.

Or so I thought.

* * *

It is said that you don't know joy until you experience sadness.

My first week in Reno was wonderful. I could love my baby and reconnect with my husband. We went to a Beatles tribute concert in Lake Tahoe with my brother. I could finally let loose, but it was really all a fraud. I was just going through the motions. Grief and pain seared through my body and the demons danced on my broken heart. That night we opened a couple bottles of wine, and I drank until I threw up.

My brother showed us around town. He took us under his wing to- make our new life in Reno as easy as possible. We are rebuilding our lives. *Why did I resist? What was I thinking?* I love it here. I love our new house.

But, I wasn't thinking. My mind was at sixes and sevens. There was too much to worry about. *What if Socks and Lily are out there somewhere, injured, not dead? They need me. All my pictures are gone. I need new clothes. What are we going to do about money? We should have taken the cats with us. I miss little Rudy. How are we going to support ourselves? Fucking Mister Room Spray. I hate him. Why did this happen to me?*

Guilt. Pain. Regret. Anger. It was all inside me. The demons were not leaving. They haunted me constantly. My mind never rested. Pain and grief were worse at night, and I needed to shut it down. I wanted to be knocked out because I didn't want to lie awake each night with anguish and panic. It was much easier to take a pill, so I willingly and purposefully chose addiction. I could no longer cope with my pain. *Screw it. I don't care. It's much better than suffering.*

I began to receive very well-intentioned care packages filled with baby clothes, gift cards, and money. The word had spread. I was in trouble. *I was a victim.* The outpouring of generosity and other people's slightly worn baby clothing was welcomed with tremendous gratitude. It also validated me as a victim. Homeless and poor, despite our college educations. We were doing okay until Katrina washed it all away. I was dressing my baby in someone else's used clothes. I was a charity case.

News coverage about the storm's aftermath and its *victims* seemed endless. *But, I am not a victim*, I thought.

"Yes, you are." Everyone told me so.

I am? I don't want to be a victim.

"But, you are a victim."

Well, I guess in theory, I am a victim.

"I never met a Katrina victim!"

Seriously? Now, I'm a celebrity?

"Were you in the floods?"

No, I wasn't in the floods. I was in the flippin' eye of the storm.

I was angry, and I began to play the victim role every day. *Here, let me show you my pictures.* I had pity parties for everything I lost. Unknowingly, it was becoming my new way of life. I was trapping myself inside a bubble inside my refugee Katrina house and blaming everything for my pain. Amidst all this turbulence, yet another addiction was quickly coming to fruition.

* * *

I still had a fear of malls. I couldn't shop for clothes. *Where do I start?* It was too problematic. I couldn't mentally process anything more difficult than a recipe. I still needed someone to tell me what to do and what I needed.

I was lying on the sofa and channel surfing, still wearing the same crappy evacuation sweatpants and t-shirt when I came across a shopping channel. The woman on QVC told me what I needed. She said that I needed a sweater, two pairs of pants because I had to have one in black and one in a color. She told me which makeup to buy, which shoes are comfortable, and to buy the Italian leather handbag. This was the answer to my mall angst. I was building a wardrobe, and I didn't need to leave the house. *Yeah!*

Packages arrived every other day. The UPS man was no longer a stranger. I joked with him. "You're at my house so much, the neighbors will start to gossip."

I bought, and I bought, and I bought. I spent more money than we had. My fear of shopping malls turned into a TV shopping addiction that was out of control. It's so embarrassing to admit it, but I relied on QVC for everything…even companionship, as my husband would spend weeks down on the Gulf Coast helping to clean up. Eventually, credit cards went into default. The creditors were calling. My FICO score plummeted. We were living paycheck to paycheck. I had a reason for every purchase. *The $700 sewing machine is a great deal!* I can make baby blankets, despite the fact I hate to sew. I knew what I was doing, and I couldn't stop. Within the haze of Ambien, I bought shit that I didn't remember purchasing until it arrived at my front door.

* * *

My new life in Reno was supposed to help me rebuild. Instead I was falling apart. I had two addictions, plus a mystery illness that kept me chronically fatigued every day for the next twelve years. My immune system was comprised. I had adrenal fatigue. I was constantly susceptible to colds and strep throat. I developed a severe headache, which I thought was a migraine. I threw up all night, my neck hurt, and I couldn't sleep. I had spinal meningitis and was quarantined for two days. My health was slowly deteriorating, yet no one seemed to believe just how badly I felt, especially my husband. I presented well. I looked good. It must be depression or PTSD.

I physically couldn't take care of my young Renee. Now, she is a toddler and required too much energy from me. Katrina was taking her early years from me, as well, but I needed her out of the house and away from me. She was too much trouble. The demons had turned my love into resentment. I couldn't care for myself, let alone a toddler.

I enrolled her in full-time daycare, but I feared the five-o'clock hour when I had to pick her up. That meant I had to feed her, bathe her, play with her, and put her to bed. She was a burden that I dreaded every day. I resented having to care for her. *I shouldn't be feeling this way. I'm a shitty mother. I want to love her, but I can't.* I was guilt-ridden. *She needs her mama, and I am abandoning her.* There were no bedtime stories or walks to the park. We didn't dance around the living room like my mother did with me. We had no tea parties. I hated myself.

Persistent stress had made my body sick, and I resented everyone who wasn't sick. I never healed from the effects of the fight or flight response of Hurricane Katrina, which began after my move to Reno. I did online research to find an answer. I had been to some ten doctors over as many years, and none of them could tell me why I was so chronically fatigued and why I had constant body pain.

I needed to find an answer to my health issues. It became my full-time job. *I must be my own advocate, my own doctor. No one knows my body better than I do.* I spent thousands of dollars on blood tests, supplements, and vitamins. They helped for a little while, but my fatigue and pain morphed into an illness that was so intense, I had moments when I couldn't walk, feed myself, shower, or switch positions in bed. The demons had taken control of my body.

Those five weeks destroyed the next twelve years of my life, my body, my mind, and my relationships. I was now in another place of hell. I was trapped inside my body and desperately wanted to get out. I was sick and tired of *being* sick and tired every day. Someone once said to me, "I don't mean to be disrespectful, but at least you don't have cancer—you're not dying." That was true, but I wasn't living either.

It was through self-reflection and the willingness to understand how my life, my health, and my relationships were being destroyed that pivoted my life. I realized that I needed to face my anguish and challenge my grief. *I must go back to Bay Saint Louis.* I wasn't rebuilding in Reno. I was deconstructing. I gained forty pounds. I felt horrible every day and couldn't engage in activities, and my relationships suffered.

My trip to the Bay completely changed my perspective. You see, Bay Saint Louis had rebuilt and moved forward. Main Street was alive with music. It was now a pretty little town with chic cafes, boutiques, and its very own yacht club. Good things were happening there. The people had moved forward as well, and they seemed happy.

Those of us who experienced the hurricane live in terms of pre-Katrina and post-Katrina; however, I had been living *in* Katrina, year after year, within my Katrina bubble inside my Katrina house in Reno. I needed to let go of the hurricane and stop self-victimizing to move forward.

That was my ah-ha moment.

I came to peace with Katrina, although it will always be a part of me in some way, yet this was my first step toward reclaiming the person inside of me—pre-Katrina.

I always held onto faith that one day my health would improve. I prayed daily that I would cross paths with a physician who could understand my illness and help me treat it. In 2017, I was referred to a Board-Certified Chiropractic Neurologist who diagnosed the sources of my chronic fatigue and pain. My illness was a result of several mitigating factors that caused my chronic fatigue syndrome: The Epstein Barre virus that lives in my thyroid; Hashimoto's thyroiditis, and a leaky gut, which allows toxins from undigested foods to travel throughout my blood system, basically poo.

My illness was real, not imagined. I spent several months in the clinic getting my illness under control through an iron-clad diet and daily brain exercises to strengthen the areas of my body that were affected. The doctor gave me the tools to heal myself, and I used those tools to regain my health rather than wallow in self-pity and hopelessness. I was desperate. I had to live again.

Slowly, I began to heal and my energy increased. I regained a productive lifestyle and began to see the possibilities of what I can do with my life going forward. I felt I was handed a miracle, and I wanted to make up for lost time, especially with Renee. I still need to be careful with stress, but I am living life.

My husband left our little family and moved back to New Orleans just as I began my clinic treatments. He is dealing with his own demons. I am now fifty-seven and a single mom. Life must change once again and, more than ever, I need to be present for my daughter.

I started a freelance editing business. It was my dream during the years I lay sick in bed, thinking about the things I would do once I was well. I am creating new friendships, and I am becoming active in women's organizations. I take my daughter camping, and we do things together daily. And, I am a co-author of this book. I've come a long way baby.

My health and my mindset were the victims. I had to do the challenging work to get through it and remain resolute and positive. I was ready to do whatever it took to get well. I wanted to live again.

My soul never gave up hope.

I no longer give victimization the power to control my life. I believe that each day will bring a fresh start with no mistakes. I have come through the maze of darkness and chaos, and I am on a new journey toward happiness and independence. There is light. Yes, I still like to shop online and on QVC, but my spending is tempered, and I still hate the malls, but I'm sleeping so much better at night now that my body has healed.

I am honored to be included in this book with amazingly strong and courageous women. I believe, as women, we experience our pain and losses in the same way. We need to rise up and share our stories to give each other a sense of validation. Life can throw many challenges our way. It is my hope that you find a little bit of yourself through my journey and know that you are not alone. You can have a good life after tragedy. Your life can turn around if you want it to. Set your course, stay strong, be courageous, and always hold onto faith. The road may be long and bumpy, but you will get to the light.

My daughter and I have moved into a beautiful new home. It is here that angels are among us. We have found a little piece of heaven.

Boo is still by my side.

Jamie Ward

Jamie Ward lives in Reno and has been an editor for some thirty years. She was an actress in theater, commercials, and movies for ten years in NYC. When the acting roles became scarce, she left the industry to join a global mutual fund company as senior editor in marketing. She loves to work with authors to help turn their manuscripts into personal masterpieces. This is her first book, launching on the anniversary of Hurricane Katrina, which proves that the darkest days will one day have light. She often dreams of traveling to Alaska to gaze at the Northern Lights while wrapped in a cozy warm blanket with a special someone.

The biggest love in her life is her sweet daughter, Renee, who gives her mama unconditional love and support and often leaves little surprises on her pillow. Her other loves and constant companions are her four kitties: Zoe, Auburn, Yuki, and Boo.

The Gift of Pain

By Dr. Danielle Litoff, MPT DPT CMP OCS CTNC

How did I get here? This is me, a mom to two amazing kids, a Doctor of Physical Therapy, celebrating my eighteen-year marriage to a great guy and an owner of my business. A very different me from my teens, twenties, and thirties.

Let's start from the beginning. I was premature. At three weeks old, I had pneumonia and was saved by boatloads of antibiotics. In 2018 we know the repercussions of antibiotics, but in 1970, they did not.

I was described as a colicky kid. My mom said I was super happy until about five minutes after I ate. Then I was miserable. This was the beginning of lifelong problems with my digestion. My parents and the medical society had no clue how to help me.

In my family, I was the cute chubby one. We ate a crappy standard American diet of Cookie Crisp cereal, PB, and J on white bread and McDonald's. I came from a Jewish family who told me, "Eat your dinner, but don't get fat." It was a very confusing message for a young girl. We never discussed what was healthy. We only spoke of beauty and being thin. That message still is something I battle with.

During my teen years, the emphasis was on low calorie and low fat. I was raised in LA, so the theme of the time was, "You can't be too rich or too thin." "Careful how much you eat, or you will get fat." The drive to be beautiful and thin and perfect on the outside was all that mattered.

I was, and still am, a competitive person. I remember my girlfriends and I had a competition to see who could eat the least.

For six months I ate only a half a head of cauliflower and a diet coke per day. I was on the swim team, swimming over twenty miles a week. I lost forty-five pounds in that year and was celebrated by my family and friends. No one ever asked about my health. No questions about why I was falling asleep in class, or why I had so many frequent colds.

In college, I started to notice issues that were quite embarrassing in the shared bathrooms of the dorms. My dorm mates would joke, "If you can't find Danielle, check the bathroom." I remember I never got a 'hangover' in the typical sense. I would get a terrible stomach ache from beer and pizza (the first signs of my gluten and dairy sensitivities).

In my nutrition class, we tracked our food for a week. I was eating less than nine-hundred calories a day and exercising hard. My diet consisted of power bars, top ramen, lettuce, and diet coke. No matter how little I ate or how much I exercised I still had a 'tummy'—it was infuriating! I had to eat less and exercise more; those were the only options I knew.

Fast forward ten years. At that point, I had been on antidepressants for four years due to anxiety and depression. Just as was every female in my family. It was very hush hush, so shameful to be on medications.

My husband and I decided it was time to start a family. I knew I needed to get off my medications to have a healthy child. I went to an acupuncturist to help with the depression and anxiety. She looked at my diet and told me it would be almost impossible to get pregnant.

This was the first time I had seen food as fuel for my body rather than the enemy. It took over two years and some diet changes to conceive, but we did! We had two perfect girls in twenty-five months.

Two pregnancies in two years was stressful on my body. Then my husband got a new job in a different state, and we moved away from family and friends. I had to leave a great job, my mothers group, and my swim team. It was so scary to leave with two small kids and start over.

Once in Reno, I started my doctoral degree. I coached the kids' soccer team, I worked thirty hours a week and competed in triathlons and masters swimming. I could be described as a type A personality. This can be a blessing and a curse. I was determined to be the best at everything I did. It kind of backfired.

I became a crazy lady, working so hard to get everything done right. I kept lists in my head because I was way too busy to write them down. I would check off things I had accomplished, but what stood out to me was what was not done. The failures and the ridiculous self-imposed expectations that were never met. There was a lack of joy in the accomplishments because I was so stressed about getting them done, perfectly so I could be valued. Good was never enough. If it was good, it had to be better next time. Every day had to be a PR (personal record), or it didn't count.

This is when my digestive issues really got ugly. No matter what I would eat, I would have a painful bloated belly that looked like I was five months pregnant. I felt like Pig-Pen from the Peanuts in a disgusting cloud, and as a physical therapist in the clinic with patients, this was mortifying.

I was exhausted. I woke up early and dragged myself to the gym because after exercise I could function. Now I know that was because I had caused my adrenal glands to become dysfunctional. I had to have the 'runners high' to be able to do anything.

A regular day looked like this:

- Get up at 4:40

- Swim from 5:30-7 a.m.

- Work ten hours

- 30-40 min workout at lunch

- Pick up the kids

- Coach soccer

- Make dinner

- Make lunches for the next day

- Do the dishes

- Put the kids to bed

- Do the laundry

- Study for school

- Crawl into bed at 11:30 p.m.

- Rinse and repeat

I lived in fight or flight mode, always running to put out a fire. Even though I ate little and exercised a lot, I still gained twenty pounds. I was so drained. I never laughed. I couldn't play, but I got shit done.

I could not find a doctor that could give me any answers or support. They would shrug and say, "You are forty, and you have two kids. Of course, you are fat and tired. Just eat less and do more cardio."

My anxiety at this point was through the roof. After dropping the girls off at day care, I remember sitting in my car in tears, just squirming in my seat. I truly wanted to crawl out of my own skin.

I would fly off the handle at my kids for the littlest of kid things, and I screamed all the time. I wanted to be perfect, so the slightest thing would throw me. One time, at my younger daughter's birthday party, we ordered a cake. I thought it was too small; my daughter accidentally dropped her piece, and I lost it. I yelled at her—at her birthday party—over a piece of cake. I still get tears in my eyes just thinking about it.

Another time I was to go on a training ride for the triathlon. The bike was the scariest part for me; I was so afraid of falling or getting hit. I believed I needed my phone just in case, but that morning it hadn't charged. I saw the dead battery and freaked. I threw the phone and started to scream and cry as I fell to the floor in a puddle. My kids and husband just stared at me in disbelief.

In 2009, I began to get reoccurring sinus infections. I had nine rounds of antibiotics in eighteen months, and I was put on five rounds of steroids. In retrospect, this worsened my gut and drained my adrenal glands.

I began to have allergies and asthma symptoms, so I was put on an inhaler. My doctors told me my immune system was failing, and I was going to be on medication for the rest of my life. She even referenced the boy in the bubble if my immune system continued at this rate.

I was killing myself to be healthy. I was eating gluten and dairy free, less than 1500 calories a day and exercising like a fiend! I was so scared and so frustrated. It made no sense, and no one could give me answers. If no one could help me, what was my life going to be like? What was going to happen to my kids?

My symptoms list looked like this

- Twenty pounds overweight

- Bloated belly

- Bathroom issues

- Exhausted in the mornings and late afternoon.

- Angry and anxious, I had no patience for anyone.

- Asthma

- Joint pain

- Nightly cravings for sugar/carbohydrates

- Feeling like a true failure

I was put on a low dose antibiotic and told this was the start. I was on that for nine months (after the nine rounds of high dose antibiotics).

I was so frustrated, I was a medical professional, working with patients to make them healthy, and I was a mess. I felt like such a fraud. How could I make recommendations for patients when I couldn't fix myself?

I had a friend who was a functional medicine chiropractor; I knew nothing of this branch of medicine. He said, "Stop this madness, I can help you."

He began to educate me on the science of food and nutrition. He did a lot of testing to determine where I was deficient in nutrients, and where my body needed help with supplements.

I began to follow the paleo diet, which restricted gluten, dairy, soy, grains, and legumes. I felt better, not 100%, but an improvement. I needed more; I wanted the why because I was losing trust in my medical doctors.

Eventually, I enrolled in a functional medicine program. The program was the beginning of my education on the gut, the root cause of my problems. I tested myself and saw in black and white where my body was breaking down. However, I still had no diagnosis.

I wanted a clearer picture of why I was doing better with strict paleo and autoimmune protocols, so I enrolled in a holistic nutrition program. This really helped me stick to the plan. I finally felt like I had some answers and I was slowly becoming empowered.

I learned that the stress was killing me and that it can be broken down to emotional, physical and environmental.

I learned that more exercise was not the answer, that long duration exercise (runs, swimming, or cycling) increases the stress hormone cortisol. Cortisol is the main hormone that regulates serotonin and dopamine, chemicals responsible for happiness.

I learned that I needed to sleep more than I needed to exercise. I did not understand that for a long time. It's still something I consciously work on.

In 2013, I had a cervical biopsy. The OBGYN thought I might have cervical cancer. The prep for the surgery was forty-eight hours of clear liquids. I lost twelve pounds, and for the first time, my stomach stopped hurting. I asked the nurse about a 10% body weight loss in forty-eight hours, but she dismissed me. This further decreased my trust in my medical providers. The interesting part was the next day my first meal was an organic chicken apple sausage with sautéed spinach and onions. I gained five pounds and four inches of bloat in less than an hour. I was at a loss.

I continued with my search for a diet to fix my problems. Paleo variations seemed to help. I went off my antidepressants because they weren't helping.

I found a functional medicine psychiatrist. She did an evaluation and full panel blood test. She found I had extremely low thyroid hormone levels and thyroid antibodies. In addition, my hormone levels were incredibly low for my age.

She told me I had Hashimoto's Thyroiditis. Finally, a real diagnosis, an explanation. It was a relief. There was an answer—something I could research, something I could 'fix'. The doctor recommended the GAPS protocol to heal my gut, so it could function properly and absorb the nutrients I needed. The protocol was developed by Natasha Campbel-Mcbride to help her son with autism, but research shows it has helped with depression/anxiety, autoimmune disease, schizophrenia, Crohn's disease, ulcerative colitis, and general IBS.

It is an elimination diet that involves six phases. Normally people can get through all six phases within a few weeks. It took me six weeks to get to stage three. Each time I tried to get to stage four my symptoms would flare.

I was so frustrated. I basically ate soup and pureed vegetables for six months. I made 100% of all my own food and carried it with me in a lunchbox every day. I could not enjoy dinners with my family or eat lunch with my friends, so I ate alone.

It was tough. The amount of time I devoted to making food was ridiculous, demanding, and isolating. I did the best I could to be prepared. I had a cooler with me 24/7, but oftentimes my family would go to dinner after the kids' games with the other families. If I had soup with me, I would bring it, but if I was out of food, I would go to the restaurant and just sit there. There was absolutely nothing I could eat, not even a salad. I felt like a freak. However, I persisted.

I continued to feel better. It took work. It took commitment. It took a change of lifestyle and thought processes. It took support and guidance. It took faith in myself to believe I was on the right path and to not give up. It took some good friends to support me and kick me in the ass when it was necessary.

I was able to get off all my prescription medications. My energy came back, my patience was better, and I found myself laughing with my kids again.

I forced myself to meditate and do yoga. I learned how to quiet my brain, so I could sleep better and exercise less.

During the healing process, I found that so many of my patients shared my experiences. They came to PT with a bad back or achy knees. I did the normal physical therapy, but then I dove deeper, asking about exercise, recovery time, sleep, and food. I got some funny looks. I'm sure they were wondering what that had to do with their achy knees.

When I applied this approach with my patients, the results were amazing. They saw improvements in their joint pain, sleep habits, and digestion.

During this time, I was working for someone else and was asked not to expand my protocol beyond the standard level of care. I felt so strongly about treating the whole system that I could not stick to standard care.

In 2015, I took a leap. With the support of my husband, father, and business partner we struck out and created Battle Born Health.

Battle Born Health is not just a physical therapy clinic. I am committed to diving deeper and discovering the answers behind why my patients are not living their lives fully.

I do not have all the answers, but I will stand in the fire with them as they walk on their journey to create a healthy life.

I know what it takes to bunk the common answers, to question the standard. I believe we all have the right to question. I do not advocate ignoring medical advice, but I do encourage second, third, and if necessary, fifth opinions when the answers given don't make sense or don't work.

This is my journey, and it continues daily. I love finding the answers that light my geeky fire. I give to others what I know to be true. I am so incredibly grateful for my pain; it has been a gift that challenges my growth and impacts the world. If one person can benefit from my story, then it has been worth it.

What I have learned so far:

1. Do your research. Your doctors can't know everything. You must know your body and your history. But, remember, WebMD did not go to medical school.

2. Stress is the primary contributor to disease.

3. Stress can be emotional, physical or environmental.

4. Sleep seven to nine hours a night. This is non-negotiable.

5. Self-care. Are you doing what you love or are you doing for everyone except yourself? Proper self-care will allow you to feel better about yourself.

6. Over-exercising creates stress. A certain amount of stress is necessary, but you will break if you overdo it.

Don't give up on yourself, ever! You are worth the work. You will have to change. Ask for help, but remember, not everyone will understand or support you. There is no magic formula; it is a puzzle with many pieces.

Every journey begins with one step no matter how small, it's the beginning.

Dr. Danielle Litoff,
MPT DPT CMP OCS CTNC

Danielle is a mom to two amazing girls and the wife of an equally amazing guy. She moved to Reno in 2007 and other than the lack of good bagels in Northern Nevada, she hasn't looked back.

Danielle loves finding movement patterns that create change and empower people with the knowledge of how to move without pain.

Dr. Litoff obtained her masters and doctoral degrees in physical therapy in 1996 and 2010. In 2010 she completed the Certification in Mulligan Concepts and was board certified in orthopaedics by the American Physical Therapy Association in 2011. She is a transformational nutrition coach (CTNC) and certified by the Kalish Institute in functional medicine.

With her education, Danielle was able to create her dream rehabilitation clinic, Battle Born Health, in Reno NV, where she can do what she loves every day.

When she is not 'working' Danielle is lucky enough to spend time with her family at the soccer field, snowboarding in the Sierras, paddle boarding in the local lakes or pushing it at the cross-fit gym.

Accidentally Moving Here
Changed My Life

By Diane Dye Hansen

Every once in a while, I reflect on my life and share my past with others using an app called Timehop. Sometimes, I get nostalgic. Other times, I roll my eyes and laugh. Right around Memorial Day, it shows me exactly how far I've come.

The post that surfaces just after Memorial Day each year asks a simple question. "Why is 'where do you live' such a hard question to answer right now?" How I went from being a six-figure marketing manager in the entertainment industry to wondering how I could afford to eat boggled my mind. Yet, there I was, writing a Facebook post from a hotel room in Reno where I was living for the week. 'Where do you live?' It was an impossible question, and it was getting more embarrassing to answer every day.

It all started in an apartment in Torrance, California. With my head hung low, I told my husband, who had been laid off two years prior, I had been let go from my job at a major video game company. With my ego dashed on the rocks, I poured myself a glass of cherry flavored UV Vodka and began my job search. As sip after sip turned into a fresh glass and more vodka, I gained confidence that my new job in the entertainment industry was just one great interview away. I continued my habit of mail-order shoes and cosmetics, so certain my lifestyle wasn't at risk. It couldn't be. My ego told me I was too good to be unemployed for long. Besides, credit cards would sustain us. We had good credit—a lot of it. My husband didn't hesitate to maintain his lifestyle either, although at a much grander level than me, getting scuba certified in Cozumel and visiting a variety of major league ballparks. He did all this while I was grinding away to make our life solvent. Yet I saw it as my responsibility to keep our boat afloat.

Resumes turned into initial interviews, which turned into second interviews. I was well on my way. You name the entertainment company, I interviewed there. And I came in second, over and over again. It got to the point where I couldn't go to a movie without getting angry when they showed the logos at the beginning of the film. With each rejection came more fear. Fear turned into more time spent over at my neighbor's house smoking weed. Poof, my problems vaporized away, and the confidence returned. I went on phone interviews, interviews, and second interviews. I came in second, again, and again. Weed turned into knocking on my neighbor's door for Xanax, sleeping instead of applying to more jobs. But, since I had the resume and contacts, I got interviews anyway.

Eventually, I was ready to go into porn. No, not doing porn. I applied to be Larry Flynt's publicist. The interview went great. I justified to myself, "Hell, if I can do a professional job communicating about porn, I can communicate about anything." I was prepared to say yes. I could see myself on private planes, going to parties, and hob-knobbing with the rich and famous.

I came in second.

Coming in second in the porn industry really made me question my worth as a professional. Still, I pressed on, assisted by alcohol and the handful of drugs I could justify doing. It scared me, but, it also gave me a peace I couldn't achieve otherwise.

Then, there was a knock on the door. It turns out debt consolidation doesn't work so well when a credit card company won't settle. I feared my phone for months. The 'reputable debt consolidation company' my husband and I hired told us to avoid creditors' phone calls and shred bills before opening. This resulted in a lawsuit landing on our doorstep. When the fateful knock came, there was only one choice to make. We had to move back to Texas to file bankruptcy. Texas was the location of a home we owned, which we had listed for sale. It was the only asset we had left, a 3,765 square foot home in a gated community on the shores of Lake Ray Hubbard. We bought it before the real estate bubble burst, with no jobs, when the banks were handing out mortgages like candy at a parade.

Even though we were back in Texas, my eyes were still trained on California. I wanted to chase the golden goose and catch it! I would say every day, between bottles of wine, "I want my life back. I want my life back!" I would daydream about having cocktails again at The Mondrian, working with celebrities, and speaking on panels at San Diego Comic-Con. I was convinced I would have it all back and more if I just stayed the course.

One day, it came. It was a phone call from the chief operations officer (COO) I used to work with when I was helping launch a film company. We had worked together before. We knew each other. We liked each other. The job as their vice president of marketing and communications was a shoe in. I jumped in my little black BMW Z3 and drove from Garland, Texas to Thousand Palms, California, where my mother-in-law Judy lived.

Finally, the day of my life-changing interview came. I was ready to nail it. After a lovely dinner with the team, the COO put her hand on my shoulder and said with certainty, "You've got this, Diane. We want you, but, we're a public company. We have to post the job." She stepped back, seeing the worry on my face, "Don't worry, the job is yours. Just give us two weeks."

Reassured, I left dinner feeling like life was coming back to me. I was going to get my life back at last! I called my husband. "Jeff! I know I am going to get this job. Call the real estate agent. Take the house off the market and let's rent it!" I was elated. I was taking action. I was on top of the world.

A few days later, my mother-in-law decided to take my dog, Porsche, for a walk on the desert trails behind her house. Night started to fall, and she wasn't back home. She had fallen, and her pelvis had shattered. Surgery and time in a convalescent home was required. One thing was certain, my dog and I couldn't be there when she returned. She couldn't have a dog running around underfoot while she was healing. I had to find another place to go. That night, I watched the movie *The Secret* for the first time. After the movie was over, I moved over to the kitchen table, bowed my head and set an intention for radical positive life change. Little did I know how much change I was about to experience.

A year prior, I picked up a freelance project as the editor-in-chief of GETAWAY Reno/Tahoe magazine. I got to know this area well by meeting business owners over the phone, writing articles, and meeting them face to face during regular area visits. The next morning, I awoke with new clarity about what I was going to do with the next two weeks. I picked up the phone.

"Andy," I took a deep breath as I spoke to my publisher. "I need a place to stay for a couple of weeks." I was certain how it would play out. I would stay in Tahoe for a couple of weeks, enjoy Reno and the surrounding area and return to Los Angeles to our former apartment on the Pacific Coast Highway, starting a new job.

I left Thousand Palms on Memorial Day weekend wearing a flowy blouse, white capri pants, and sandals. I arrived in South Lake Tahoe to snow. I took a happy selfie, amused by the novelty of it all. This is not the first story I have heard where snow signified a new beginning.

Memorial Day turned into my birthday, June 3rd. A week later, I was on the patio of a restaurant in South Lake Tahoe called Riva Grill. With the sun beaming down, I was enjoying their specialty drink, a Wet Woody, with my team. My phone vibrated. I had an email. It was from the COO. This was it.

Hi Diane,

It was a pleasure meeting with you a few weeks ago. We posted the position of vice president of marketing communications. You are absolutely excellent, and I would love to work with you again but…

My heart skipped a beat.

One of the candidates who applied had a master's degree.

I had a bachelor's in business administration.

We decided to go with that candidate. All the best to you and where you land. I'm sure it will be somewhere wonderful.

I screamed the F-word at the top of my lungs on the very tourist-packed patio. People turned toward me in horror. I felt the concern, shock, and disdain of those around me. Time froze. I didn't just start crying. I began to wail! Tears flowed down my cheeks like a waterfall after a good winter. Embarrassed, I rushed to the bathroom to hide. I felt like a turtle flipped over on its shell, little legs waving. The tears didn't stop for hours. I was stuck. I couldn't go back to California. I didn't have any interviews or job prospects there. I didn't even have a place to stay. I couldn't go to Dallas. I barely had the gas money and, if I went there, what would I do? The house was for sale! I felt powerless, hopeless, and beaten.

My husband gave me a $400 a month, maximum, to spend on a place to live. Being from Texas, I had no idea what I was facing. I was positive I could find a place, month to month, that would help me bide my time. I was dead set on applying to jobs in California and driving down to interview. I would find a way! But I had a dog, a dog who was my world. My pets were the closest thing I had to children.

The first place I looked at was Echo Summit. To this day, I drive by, and it looks like something you would see in a gory horror movie. The caretaker of the place was just as syrupy creepy. When I drove up, the place was littered with rusty tools. The lanky caretaker lumbered out and addressed me. "Are you here about the room?" His speech was slow and drawn out, adding to the horror movie ambiance of the situation. It looked like an old motel which was being converted, albeit at a glacial pace, into apartments. He swung the door open. "The current residents are still here, but they will be checking out soon." A cat leapt ominously from the bed and ran out the door. He wanted me to walk in first. I peeked in. The place had tattered curtains and reeked of cat urine. "Oh, I see," I said. "Thank you!" I have never high-tailed it out of anywhere faster, except for my next location.

I saw a roommate-wanted ad and emailed a person named Dana. I didn't think to question male or female. When I drove up to the house, I saw that Dana was decidedly male, and looked a little bit like the old porn star Ron Jeremy, a sturdy but short guy with a mustache wearing a white tank top and long boxer shorts. I breathed, tried to stay positive, and walked up to introduce myself. Dana was nice enough. It was the large German Shepherd dogs who wouldn't stop humping me and the uncleaned spots of dog mess that broke my spirits about the place. It felt highly uncomfortable and wrong in more ways than I could count.

I kept looking. The weekly motels were twice my price range. The hopeless feeling grew. I went from miracle seeking to flat out inaction. Porsche and I wore out our welcome at my team member's house and I was seriously considering buying a tent.

Seeing my struggle, my publisher spoke up. "Diane, if you need to stay with us, you can." My publisher lived in Gardnerville, in a nice house by a park. The arrangement was perfect for my dog and I. Best, I felt emotionally held and supported. Over the years, Andy and his wife Tiffany had become less like bosses and more like family. Little did either of us know that I would end up living in their guest bedroom for four months. People would ask me where I lived, and I didn't know how to answer. I was firmly in what I now call the 'hallway of life'. I didn't see any light under the doors, but I kept moving forward.

When I spoke to my husband, our conversations were mostly centered around my financial progress. What was I doing to grow my business? Was I looking for a full-time job? How could I make more money to support the household and get our lives back on track?

Slowly, with awareness of my situation, increased consciousness because daily drinking was no longer part of my life, and my refusal to beat myself up over the state of my existence, things started to come together. I started to pick up freelance writing clients. I gained confidence. I got to know myself as a person, not simply as a wife or someone's employee. I escaped the veil of needing to perform for people, and I started to relish the simple pleasures in life. I turned extreme deal shopping and couponing for food into something that was fun. Joy was my daily medicine.

One day, I answered a posting on Craigslist for a writer. I nailed the interview and got the job. I was stunned to discover my new boss appeared in *The Secret*. Life had come full circle from that moment at the kitchen table in Thousand Palms, when my last hope was hanging by a thread, and I was begging the universe for change. Although my job wasn't in the entertainment industry, I had landed in the personal development industry. I developed an appreciation for the shift. I started my new position, and it all came back. My salary was back. I rented a nice, pet-friendly apartment. I could afford to feed myself and even treat myself to a present every now and then. Only now, instead of entitlement, I felt something new. It was gratitude.

I remember calling my husband. "Come up to Carson City, honey," I said. "It's all fixed." However, when Jeff came back, I noticed what had been there all along. I had justified the abuse that was taking place in my relationship because it was part of daily life. Most of the time, things were great, and Jeff was my best friend. But when it was bad, it was bad. The cutting comments were sprinkled throughout the day. After not living with it for four months, the abuse was obvious. I started to drink more. Money got tight again as our lifestyle became comfortable and gambling became entertainment. It was more obvious that I was the sole wage earner and had been for three years. I realized, despite this, that he controlled all the money.

However, the open and welcoming nature of Reno and Carson City did something for me. I had developed relationships he didn't have a part in. I realized I had been isolated for years. I had money of my own and it was hard for him to keep tabs on all of it when I was in another state. Because I had relationships, I also had a support system who would stand by me. People ask abused women all the time why they stayed. For me, it was because the abuse was my normal—until it wasn't. It was normal for a man to have sex with me in my sleep. It was normal to be pinched when I said something he didn't like. It was normal to have an allowance and ask for money. It was normal for him to have full veto rights on my friends. It was normal to give birth to my daughter at age twenty-seven, having no choice but to give her up for adoption. It was normal to stick my head in the sand. It was all normal until it wasn't. Four months living without him broke through my ceiling of denial. It was like taking the red pill in the movie *The Matrix*.

I didn't want to wake up. This area created my new normal.

One day, I decided it was time to have a serious (and possibly dangerous) discussion with my husband. I told him, "If we are going to discuss our marriage, you need to get all the guns out of the house." The way he used to leave his guns out would terrify me. Walking on eggshells becomes like walking on glass when a weapon is inches away during an argument, and I avoided arguments at all cost. I suggested he take the guns to his mother's house.

Before he left, he said, "You know, my mom thinks if I leave, you will lock me out."

Honestly, until he said that, I wasn't even considering it. I asked my new support system, could I do it? Could I leave? Tiffany said she would sit with me after I locked him out and would be ready to call the police if he tried to come back.

The next day, Jeff loaded up the trunk of the BMW Z3 with as many guns and ammunition as it could handle. He filled it to the brim but still had to leave one .22 behind. After he was at his mother's house, I called him to tell him to not come back. Initially, I said I needed a break, but the longer I experienced life without abuse, the more I never wanted to go back to that life. I have not seen him face to face since that day in early 2012. We divorced in 2013.

Jeff was always convinced I would come back. He called my time away my "Rumspringa," referring to the time where Amish youth go out into the world and make a decision to leave forever or join the community for life. I left forever. It was a bit of a Rumspringa at first, with plenty of dates, rum, and other drinks, and some poor choices. However, in the end, the community I returned to was the community of self-awareness and a commitment to making a difference in the world.

Today, the only thing that is the same about my life is my best friend who saw it all go down and has been by my side since 1999. I stopped using drugs and alcohol as the solution to all my problems in 2014. Life hasn't been a total bed of roses. Or, maybe it has been because it hasn't been without thorns. My dog Porsche died in 2016. The same year, I was laid off from my job four months into my master's program. Instead of quitting school, I restarted my company.

Every day has been a new beginning since I arrived in Nevada in 2011. Today, I live life one day at a time. I know if I do the right thing today, tomorrow will work itself out. I own a consulting firm which helps organizations in crisis or transition identify opportunity and take action to create results. I have a team of skilled professionals behind me and a host of friends who support me. The relationships I have had, since then, have all helped me grow. Not one of them has been abusive. Not one has led me to drink or use drugs. I am grateful.

All of this did not come automatically. I had a lot of work to do on myself and how I communicate. It's an ongoing process. I realized my story does not own me or control the decisions I make. I can help others with my experience, but it doesn't have to drive me into reaction, fear, or overwhelm. I am stronger because of my past, but it doesn't define me.

Every time life does its thing; I remember my power rests within the pauses I take, the questions I ask, and knowing what I can control—myself. Visualization is important, but much more powerful when grounded in consistent, focused, action, and clarity. This realization prompted me to create Critical Opportunity Theory, which shows people how they can transform problems into opportunity. I call the lighter side of this theory Crappertunity™. To this day, when someone asks me why I moved to Nevada, I tell them I accidentally moved here. It was my Crappertunity™ moment, and it was the best moment of my life.

Diane Dye Hansen

Diane is the founder and president of What Works Consultants Inc., a consulting firm which helps organizations transform challenges into opportunity through business consulting and human resource recruiting. She created Critical Opportunity Theory during her Master of Communication Management program at the University of Southern California, Annenberg School for Communication and Journalism. The research-based theory identifies what causes individual and organizational decline and how to transform those issues into opportunities. Her column appears weekly at CarsonNow.org, and her radio show can be heard on KNVC 95.1. A documentary about her theory is being produced by the Divine Spirit Network.

She was raised by her single mother, Barbara, who post-divorce, had to reinvent herself at age forty-seven. It was from her mother that Diane learned about second chances, resilience, and the power of personal intention. This story is dedicated to her.

Damaged Goods

By Renee Cooper

It was June, the summer in between my freshman and sophomore year in high school. My family and I had just moved to a larger town in Southern Idaho.

I had gotten my first real job at the only fast food restaurant in town, Arctic Circle. After working there for three weeks, I went to collect my first paycheck. I was excited as I walked in. On my off days, I babysat my baby niece for my older sister. On this particular day, she happened to be with me when I went to pick up my check.

My boss handed me my check as he looked at me and shook his head. The kids that were working that day laughed and said, "Renee, now we see why you had to move here."

I was clueless. *Why would they say that?* I left with my check and my niece.

The next day when I went back to work my shift, a girl came up to me and asked, "So, you have a baby?"

I was shocked. I told her no, it was just my niece. She said, "Sure, I heard her call you Mama."

Then, she just went back to work.

The summer came to an end. I began my sophomore year at my new school. I was nervous as I walked down the halls (like any new student is on the first day). The school was huge compared to the tiny one I had come from. People pointed at me in the hallways and laughed. I didn't understand what they were laughing about.

I chose not to overthink it; I just smiled and walked by.

Right away I started getting a lot of interest from upperclassman boys—the juniors and seniors. They would ask me out on dates. I was extremely excited about that but told them I was only fifteen; I wasn't allowed to date yet. They would say, "Sure," and raise their eyebrows and laugh. This thoroughly confused me. I had no idea why they would say that.

A month into school I was asked by multiple people to go to a party. I knew my mom wouldn't allow me to go, but wanting to fit in somehow and wanting to make friends, I lied and told her I was staying the night at a girlfriend's house. That night at the party I found myself really drunk after only two beers.

I got really dizzy and felt sick. I ran upstairs to the bathroom, barely making it in before everything came up. Dizzy and disoriented, I crawled to a bedroom to lie down. Before I knew it, I was out cold. I remember hearing the door open and close; I thought someone was just checking on me.

I woke up to a heavy weight on top of me, someone grunting and pulling down my pants. I wiggled and struggled as I said, "No, get *off* me!"

He said, "Shut up, it's not like you've never done it before, you whore. You have a kid."

Then he punched me.

I must've blacked out or went into shock, because I just lay there, not moving. I remember it seeming like hours had passed. Then, he just left. I lay there a few minutes more.

My entire body hurt, and I was still very sick. I puked on the carpet. Then, I pulled my pants up over my legs, thinking, *why are my legs so sticky?*

I went into the bathroom, and I saw my swollen face as my eye was already starting to turn black.

I snuck out of the house and stumbled to my car. I drove home and quietly snuck into my room. Obviously, I didn't want to wake my sleeping parents and have them see me like this. It was three o'clock in the morning when I went into my bathroom and looked down at my legs. They were covered in dried blood.

I sat in a hot bath and silently cried for the rest of the night.

The next morning, I got up and put makeup on to cover my black eye and cheek. I couldn't tell my parents because I was so ashamed of myself. All I knew to do was to take the blame for what happened to me. It was my fault, I should have never lied and went to the party, and now I felt like damaged goods.

I put on my sunglasses and left the house. I got on my horse and rode all day. I'm pretty sure I rode and cried for eight hours straight.

I went back to school the following Monday, again to people looking at me, laughing, and making comments. One girl did ask me if I was the one that puked in her room with mean squinty eyes. I quickly apologized and left.

My sophomore year went by with me keeping my head down and working. I pushed it all down and never talked about what happened to anyone. All I could do was continue with my life ignoring the fact that I was changed forever. My innocence lost, with that I felt different inside, I no longer liked myself. When I looked in the mirror I saw this strange person I didn't know.

I found myself seeking out the 'bad' kids, the ones that got in trouble, the ones that didn't follow the rules. The ones I didn't have to answer to. I never showed weakness and never cried again.

I created this strong independent persona that seemed, from the outside, to have it all together. That was cool and fearless, that could take on anything and win.

However, inside, I was scared of everything and everyone. I knew no one would like me if they knew the truth, that I was damaged goods. I would intentionally put myself in situations that could harm me. I would drive drunk or pass cars on the wrong side of the road. Friends would think I was either fun or crazy. I didn't care enough to take care of myself. I knew that if I got hurt or died, that I deserved it.

With my parents, I played the sweet little girl they always knew and loved. I passed all my classes, worked, and helped out around the house. As long as I didn't rock the boat, no one would notice how damaged I was. No one would ask any questions. And no one did, ever.

My junior and senior years passed. After graduation, I focused on one thing—getting out of that town. I wanted to run and start fresh where no one knew me. So, I worked two jobs and saved up all I could. I left for college three-hundred miles away.

Once at college, I rolled right into the same patterns. Running with the fast crowd, taking risks and putting myself in the wrong places all the time. I should have died a hundred times my first year in college. I would date strangers, hitchhike, and drive my car across half frozen lakes.

You name it; I did it.

I would *only* date the bad boys. The nice guys made me feel good and worthy, and I knew if I fell for one I would have to come clean and tell him how damaged I was. I made sure those relationships never lasted long.

I continued to play the part of this fun, crazy, adventurous girl that always made sure everyone around her was okay. I never wanted to disappoint or upset anyone ever. Yet, that is what I always expected and wanted for myself, hurt and disappointment, because that is what damaged goods get.

I dropped out of college three times; when things started to go well, I would quit and run.

I was convinced that I could never let anyone know the true me, the damaged me.

During my senior year of college, I was looking for a change, and knew the guy I was dating was getting more serious than I wanted to be. I started a fight in my car on our way to visit his mother during spring break. We were right outside Reno, where my sister and her family had just moved. I was driving, and after he began name calling and yelling, I drove into the airport, pulled his bags out of my car and threw them on the sidewalk. As he got out to get his bags I drove away. That was sure to make him hate me and end our relationship.

It worked.

I headed to my sisters in Reno. This was the tool I had learned to use to avoid conflict. All I had to do was simply run away.

I got a job the following weekend as a personal trainer in Reno. There, I fell into the pattern of dating the wrong guys, again.

I dated one that was married just because I knew that would never last. After about nine months, I felt things were going a bit too well. So once again, I ran. This time I ran to Sun Valley, Idaho.

I got an audit job where I could work all night and ski all day. I had fallen right back into self-sabotage. It lasted all winter.

April came. I was so thin and sick, that I landed myself in the local hospital.

It was there that a nurse looked at me and said that if I continued down the path I was going, I would be dead in six months. She sat and held my hand and asked me why I was killing myself.

It was then that I cried for the first time since I was fifteen.

I told her what happened and told her who I had become because of it. She held me, and we talked for hours. The next day she brought me a book to read. I don't remember the name of the book, but it said that the greatest gift we can give ourselves is to forgive ourselves for not being perfect.

I read the entire book in the three days I was in the hospital. When I was released, I called my sister to see if I could move back in with her family in Reno. I was twenty-one. I wanted to try something new and go back.

I moved back to Reno and got a great job at a lighting company. I met new friends and coworkers; they were all much older than me, and I felt safe with them. I went back to personal training at the gym I had worked at before. I was making good money, and for the first time, I thought about my future.

One day, I met a couple of guys at the gym. They both seemed nice. One of them, a cowboy, was more interested in me than I was in him. The other was just a nice guy. I wanted a relationship with someone that I could see a future with.

At this point in my life, I still did not trust myself. The best thing I knew to do was to introduce both guys to my sister.

Her advice was to date the guy that was the cowboy. He was blonde with blue eyes, and she liked him best. I have to admit that he talked a good talk and we definitely had fun dating. I just never felt that he was the *right* guy; something was off.

The fall after I turned twenty-two, we moved in together. Slowly, over time, red flags began popping up. He would leave for days and not come home, and he started drinking more. Sadly, he was also using drugs.

I knew he was not the forever guy for me. I was planning to leave when, after living together for six months, I found out that I was pregnant. I told him, and he said I should have an abortion. Then, I told my mom and sister, and they both suggested that I should talk to him about marriage.

I'm not sure why I still did not trust myself, but I didn't. So, acting on the advice of both my mom and sister, I told my boyfriend that I would not have an abortion and that I thought we should get married.

He hesitantly said okay.

We got married three months later.

The abuse started on our wedding night. Our hotel room had a hot tub, and I told him that I couldn't use it while pregnant. In a drunken rage, he threw me into the hot water and raped me.

Once again, I felt like damaged goods.

I was right back to that scared little fifteen-year-old girl, but this time I had a child to think about.

The next day when he woke up, I had left and gone back to the little house we shared. I packed all of my things and was ready to leave. He showed up upset, apologizing for his behavior. I reminded him of what he did, but he didn't think what had happened was rape because we were married. He also said that if I left him he would take our child, and I would never see it again.

He reminded me that his dad was a millionaire, and he could go wherever he chose. I was so ashamed for once again putting myself in this situation.

I didn't tell anyone what happened, and I ultimately decided to stay.

Seventeen years and a total of three kids. I stayed because I was damaged goods—because this was what I believed I was worth.

I had forgotten all about that book I read, about forgiveness and forgiving myself. Then, in 2006, I was given the book, *The Secret*.

I devoured it and began reading more books like it. I started growing, setting goals, and having dreams again. I started believing that I was worth more and that my children deserved to see me happy. I took my three kids and filed for divorce on August 29, 2007.

I call this *my* Independence Day.

After my Independence Day, I continued to read and grow. I reached out for help to overcome my past, and I created lists of all the great things I deserved. Including what the perfect partner would be for me.

Today, I'm married to a wonderful 'nice guy', the guy I never thought I deserved. He knows my past and loves me unconditionally.

If I could go back and talk to that sweet, young fifteen-year-old girl, I would tell her to love herself enough to reach out for help. I would say, "Forgive yourself for not being perfect, trust your gut, know that we never lose, we just learn from our mistakes." Most importantly, there is no such thing as damaged goods when it comes to human experiences. They are experiences to grow and learn from.

Renee Cooper

Renee lives in Reno, Nevada with her husband, Brian. Together, as a blended family, they have five children and one-and-a-half granddaughters.

Renee is a wellness educator and medical empath, teaching alternatives to chemical-based products and natural medications. She also works at B3 Prosperity Partners as a financial planner where she specializes in working with women to create financial certainty and security, so they have the power and freedom to take care of themselves.

She created TriBE, a women's empowerment group where women encourage, lift each other up, and support each other in every aspect of their lives.

Renee and Brian are land developers of a green, sustainable community called Triple B Ranch Estates. She surrounds herself with incredible people that believe and support her in her vision and mission. Renee is a true believer of the power of paying it forward by lifting others up first.

Rising from the Abyss

By Ly Smith

I was slumbering peacefully in my comfortable, Tempurpedic mattress when my eyes shot open. I started hyperventilating, feeling trapped and claustrophobic inside of my own head. I sat up in the darkness in my rather large master bedroom, and still I couldn't shake off the suffocating experience. I heard my inner voice screaming, *I can't breathe! I'm trapped! Must escape! Get me out of here!* I tried to calm the voice with my conscious thoughts of, *I'm okay, I'm okay. Just breathe, in and out. I'm safe, I'm all right.* As I fought the confusion and disorientation, I walked downstairs, opened my sliding glass door, and fully breathed in the night air. *Is this what a panic attack feels like? What is going on?*

I've always considered myself an optimistic, happy-go-lucky, cheerful gal. I never encountered a lot of stress. After all, I was living my dream of being a stay-at-home mom, and I had practically everything I needed. I was living in a beautiful home with my husband of fourteen years, his nineteen year-old-son, and our twelve-year-old daughter. I had time freedom that would make most people envious. I had a balanced life between marriage, motherhood, and time with girlfriends. So, how did I end up in a downward spiral of depression?

It seemed like I woke up one evening in a panic, when really it was a slow road of neglect. I neglected to pay attention to my heart that desired connection. I neglected to maintain the communication with my husband that had been key to our marriage. I neglected my health and stopped caring about what I was feeding my body. I neglected my mind that was hungry for new knowledge regarding personal development, psychology, and intellectual entertainment.

Perhaps the downward spiral began the night I had a conflict with my husband, Robert, that left me distraught over how to stay married and respect myself at the same time. I didn't like how it seemed that my stepson was treating the family and our house shortly after his eighteenth birthday. My observations were that he was not participating in any family activities, and he was not cooperating with my simple house rules and chore requests. He was coming and going as he pleased without any communication, and he did not show any courtesy toward anyone. While I was in support of him staying with us so he could save money to afford a move to Southern California, I also had expectations.

I think I gave Robert the impression that I just wanted his son kicked out of the house. Honestly, I did want that if he was going to continue what I perceived to be inconsiderate and uncooperative behavior. I wanted Robert to put me first and communicate that to his son. I went as far as to say, "He is my stepson, I am his step-mom, I get it that he is going to treat me in any way he likes. However, first and foremost, I am your wife, and it pains me that you are willing to let anyone on the face of this planet treat me with such disrespect. What does that communicate to me about your level of respect for me?"

In the heat of the moment, Robert responded, "It just seems like all you want is for me to kick him out. I will kick you out before I kick him out."

I was dumbfounded at what I was hearing. What was I to do with that information? How was that meant to make me feel? I only remember thinking to myself, *I have way more self-respect than this. Do I walk out (of the marriage after fourteen years) because of this?*

For days that turned into months, I struggled because I love my husband, and he has so many great traits and contributions. He had been my best friend before we fell in love. He had been my rock whenever I wrestled the tough times in life. He had been my greatest supporter, making my dreams come true. He had provided for the family through his dedication and hard work.

There was a moment in our courtship that Robert was expressing his love to me. I was in North Carolina visiting my friends and family, and we were conversing on the phone. He was sharing a car analogy in relation to trust, and the heartfelt intimacy reached my core in such a way that I found myself awestruck, with tears streaming down my cheeks. He had reached a depth within me where no one had gone before, and it was so sincere and genuine. I was quite breathless in those seconds.

All these years later, I felt that same depth of my core ripping in heartbreak like a knife tearing through a burlap curtain. Though I had been gunny sacking our issues and challenges, I also had faith that we could overcome anything. For the first time, a seed of doubt had found good ground within my heart and mind and took root.

I was going through the motions of daily life like a tedious spider spinning her web mindlessly, weaving one task to the next. I would wake up at 5 a.m. Tuesday through Friday, make the coffee, cook up breakfast and pack a lunch for my husband. I would send him out the door by 5:45a.m., then sort out my thoughts for the day before waking my daughter for school. I would drive her to the campus and return home to either crawl back in bed or start my daily chores. I loved playing mom, but I detested being a housewife because cleaning house was definitely not my thing. I would often distract myself with social media and mobile games like Candy Crush or Solitaire for hours on end. Around 3 p.m., I would head out to pick up my daughter and carpool, depending on the day. I would stop by the grocery store on the way home to pick up items for dinner, so I could have it close to ready by the time my husband would return from his job. I would greet him at the door with a hug and kiss, just like I had done nearly every day I had been a stay-at-home mom.

The family would dine together most evenings. Afterward, our daughter would put on a show on Netflix. I would curl up on my corner of the couch, where I would cozy up under my favorite blanket. Robert would stay at the dining table on his laptop to write a Yelp review or follow the latest current event on social media, a hobby that allowed him to share the critiques from his analytical mind, vent his restless thoughts or feed his desire to debate. Later, our daughter would head to bed, and I would return to a mobile app game or pull up a book on my Kindle until my eyes could not stay open. The night would wipe the web away, and I would repeatedly spin without much joy, without any fulfillment.

The panic attack per se forced me to wake up to my situation. I knew I wasn't happy, I knew I was confused and lost, I knew I was getting sick and tired of being sick and tired. I just didn't know what to do about it because I didn't know what I really wanted. I felt stuck in my sense of duty and obligation as a wife. After all, I vowed for better or for worse, till death do us part. What does that really mean? Was this as good as it was going to get? What would happen when we became empty-nesters? Was there anything to look forward to? Was I actually considering leaving my marriage? Was it better to leave my marriage with my self-respect intact or was it better to stay, wondering if I would ever see the satisfaction of being first in the eyes of the man to whom I had given my heart and life?

Do I do the right thing, or do I do what makes me happy? Do I tough it out for the next four years until our daughter leaves for college...or is

*life too short even to endure four years? Is this just a phase? Am I dealing
with a mid-life crisis? What is wrong with me?*

I felt so disconnected…from my marriage, from my daughter,
from my stepson, from my friends, from my life, and worst of
all—from myself. I didn't know who I was anymore. So much of
my identity had been wrapped up in taking care of my family and
my home. I knew the love language of my husband, I knew what
would make my daughter happy, I knew what would appease my
stepson, and yet, I was clueless to my own interests, curiosities,
passions. It didn't help that I wasn't sharing any of my despair
with anyone. All those swirling questions I kept to myself. The
seed of self-doubt was becoming a sapling, nourished by my
apathy and lethargy. I was camouflaging it with a smile and
cheerful disposition, so no one could see that I didn't really have
it together.

For nearly two years, I dug deep within myself to sort out my
truth, discover who I really am, and explore what intrigued or
piqued my interest. I made a New Year's resolution at the
beginning of 2017 to think only of myself until I understood the
desires of my heart. I chose the word "laugh" as my word for the
year because I could not remember when I last broke out in
effusive laughter. I figured if laughter is the best medicine, I was
willing to down it as much as possible to cure my ails. Initially, I
struggled with guilt and feeling selfish, but my desire to take care
of myself overpowered those reactive emotions. I had heard of
self-care and its importance as a wife and mother, but I didn't
really get it until I really got it.

I started with a day at a local spa to celebrate a girlfriend's
birthday. I had never been to the spa before, and I savored every
moment, from the time with my girlfriend by the pool, in the wet
sauna and the dry sauna, in the hot tub, to my massage and facial

that left me rejuvenated and refreshed beyond the surface. I returned home feeling revitalized and wanting more.

The next several months, I attended a weekly improv group who left me in stitches, my cheeks rising higher along with my spirits throughout the sets, and my sides aching with pleasure. To help me pass the lowliest and loneliest of times, I would watch reruns of my beloved sitcom, *Friends*. I could recite most of the lines of just about any episode, and I would still chuckle hundreds of times over. During that season of my life, every little bit made a difference.

I attended a monthly women's networking luncheon in search of quality female friendships. It was there I found a coach who helped me find clarity, a mission, and eventual purpose that pulled me through the abyss to where I could feel like I could walk on water and ride waves of success and prosperity. I was also a member of a tribe of women who surrounded me with unconditional love and support unlike anything I had ever experienced in my life. They were women willing to accept me exactly as I was, listen to my broken heart, lend shoulders for me to cry upon, envelop me in nonjudgmental embraces, and lift me up into the light of their beautiful essences. Through their genuine friendship and sincere sisterhood, I was able to tread on that seed of self-doubt before it bloomed, and till new ground in my mind and heart for blossoms of possibilities.

I began seeking books, videos, podcasts, and music that would feed my soul with positive wisdom, my mind with thought-provoking psychology, and my vibes with pulsating rhythms. I journaled to let my inner self vent frustrations, seek inquiries, and share what little joys I could implore. I felt like I was molting the mask that held me bound and stepping into a new self who was nothing but a vibrant and brilliant energy. I was finally freeing myself of chains of hopelessness and bonds of despair, of fear and mistrust.

Yet, I wasn't sharing any of it with Robert, mostly because I feared his rejection and criticism. With him, I was still experiencing an emptiness and mediocre existence. I didn't trust him with any of my vulnerabilities. I didn't convey anything beyond what I deemed absolutely necessary. I didn't believe in him and I didn't believe in us. I was barely beginning to believe in myself.

I had heard a story on NPR about picking five personality traits or behaviors that are non-negotiable, annoy the heck out of you, and making sure the people you want to be with don't have them. The story seemed to tie in with Robert's question regarding me settling for him. Did I value him? Had I settled for him? If I did, what was I supposed to do about it? While it seemed like I was moving onward and upward in one area of my life, I was still tethered to my troubled marriage. What made us, *us*? What made us good? If he was who he was, and I was who I was, and neither of us was going to change, what was the point of keeping us together? If I felt so done with that chapter of my life, how would I close it and write the epilogue?

I wasn't very kind during this time of pondering. I couldn't look Robert in the eye and tell him that I wanted to fight to keep us together. I just wanted to fight, and I wasn't fair about it, cutting him with words and putting him down again and again. Many times, my thoughts were elsewhere, or on the things I perceived he wasn't getting right. I knew I was supposed to be mindful of his goodness and be grateful for anything I could cherish, but I really lacked the desire to bother trying. Any effort I did invest into seeing the good was immediately replaced with distrusting certainty that the good was temporary and would lead to disappointment.

In a desperate move, we sought the help of a marriage and family therapist. However, it seemed to make matters worse as we fought more than ever. The painful energy was palpable and even pushed our daughter away.

For months, I was dying in a fire of heartache and withdrawal. I was sharing a roof and utilities with a stranger who I previously considered my best friend. I couldn't carry a conversation beyond small talk because I couldn't find any common ground. I felt I had lost him to the internet, where he devoured debates with acquaintances who fed his intellect. I often called that technology "the other woman," that could seduce my husband time and time again, while I could do nothing to gain his attention. In moments when he would reach out, I brushed him off in my stubbornness and pride, pushing away the very interaction I starved for most. It felt like we carved a canyon too wide and too deep, too impossible to cross and ever unite again, especially if we were walking in opposite directions. And we were rapidly losing the will to continue.

During those same months, I was rising out of the ashes of my depression into a level of greatness I had never known about myself. A dream I had carried within me for over twenty years reawakened, a dream to be an international public speaker. I discovered a clarity for my purpose, mission, and vision. I learned I had a talent for initiating clever conversations with business owners that led to creative collaborations. While hope for my marriage seemed to be a hidden treasure lost within a maddening map leading nowhere, it was concurrently designing a business plan that shined like a rare gem.

As 2017 was nearing its end, I wondered if my marriage was journeying toward the same. There was no glimpse of even a faded star, nor a tunnel of passage through which we might find a miracle. Still, in November, Robert and I spent a day in New York City, followed by an eleven-day cruise through the southern Caribbean islands and back to Miami. With no responsibility to friends or family, I told Robert I didn't want to socialize with anyone on the ship but focus on getting us reconnected. I knew I had to truly give of myself if I was going to do my part to resuscitate what seemed like a single breath of life we had together. The time was awkward in moments, but I found a time and place to open up a few sentences about my business. And he was intrigued. After some time, I shared more details, and he was interested.

Once we returned home, I opened up to give him about a paragraph worth of my experiences with my entrepreneurial journey. He was enthusiastic. That led me to share my daily victories, and he expressed excitement. I enjoyed receiving his support, and I reciprocated with gratitude.

At the turn of 2018, it seemed I was manifesting what I called fireworks every day, so much prosperity was happening so fast! My depression passed, and I thrived in a glorious resurrection of passion. In January, I opened an office in a beautifully restored building by a river. In February, I became an international bestselling author in a collaborative book. I also took command of my health, slimming away seventeen pounds and restoring my energy. In March, I attended Brendon Burchard's High Performance Academy, where I was affirmed in my diligent discipline. It was there I gained an appreciation for my husband— my heart bursting with immense love. His abundant support allowed me to fully experience the knowledge and joy I took away from the long weekend. Additionally, I advanced in a Toastmasters International competition and graduated in a Dale Carnegie Skills for Success course.

In April, Robert and I celebrated our seventeenth wedding anniversary, it was the best one yet. We were communicating better, we were more connected, we grew more intimately. Finally, my soul, my business, and my marriage were in alignment, and I was laughing with delight!

Gone are the nights when I would wake up in suffocation and despair, struggling to find my next breath and keep moving. In place have come nights when my head rests upon the pillow, satisfied with the tasks attempted and completed, and I can breathe deeply in gratitude for the lives I've touched and those who have touched mine. My heart beats full of joy and abundant love. I've moved beyond the confusion and disorientation to a place of immense clarity, confidence, and faith. I have risen into a fully charged life that is unstoppable! Is this what it feels like when a phoenix takes flight?

Ly Smith

Ly Smith is a collaborative author of the international best-seller The Real Journey of the Empowered Mom Boss. After fulfilling her dream of being a stay-at-home mom, she ventured to the next chapter of her life as an entrepreneur.

She turned her passion for creating collaborations into the prosperous venture, B2B Matched, as a small business concierge helping entrepreneurs expand their networks and enhance their net worth. Ly is a graduate of a Dale Carnegie's Skills for Success, an award-winning Toastmaster, public speaker, and success coach.

She enjoys hiking, cooking ethnic dishes, dancing, and travel. She lives in Reno with her husband and daughter.

I Am THAT Person

By Susan Ackerman

How can this still get to me after thirty years? It happened so long ago and yet every time I think about it … I mean *really* think about it, I fall apart as if it were yesterday.

I was talking to my daughter Heather tonight (she's a therapist— living in Tacoma Washington), and I was sharing with her my angst in writing this chapter. Trying to figure out what to write about, what chapter of my last fifty-four years I needed to share, what would speak to people, what story would make a difference? I know I have a lot I could share. My life has been one giant saga— both good and bad— but I feel I have moved forward, put the past in the past, healed my gaping wounds, and moved onto a new beginning. I started going through each chapter of my life, one by one in search of the 'right chapter'. The one chapter that would scream out and say YES, this is it. This is the story you need to share. This is where you need to go. Over and over I would go through the litany of events and veto each one; abusive childhood? In the past. Alcoholic parents? In the past. Abusive first marriage? In the past. The loss of a child? In the past. Divorce? In the past? Second marriage? In the past.

At each segmented reality of my life, I declared myself healed. I just wasn't feeling it. Convinced that I had moved on from each and every area of my past, I explained to my daughter that they just weren't the right stories. She didn't buy it. After a few minutes of conversing about the different areas of my life, assuring her that I was past everything that had happened, and had fully moved on to a new life— her reaction was: "Oh, you're THAT person."

Huh? What person? I literally had no idea what she was talking about. She giggled a little— you know, one of those giggles that says, "I know something you don't know," and then preceded to hang up the phone to eat dinner. It was one of those twilight zone moments when you look around the room and think, *what just happened?* I shook my head and went to the refrigerator, still wondering what kind of person she was talking about.

It's funny how sometimes the simplest conversations can lead to the most profound awareness. I couldn't get her words out of my mind. *That Person.*

A few nights ago, at the suggestion of a friend, I watched a movie called *The Shack*. My understanding was that this movie centered around a man who, through behaviors of his own choosing, had hit rock bottom, was in danger of losing everything in his life, and rediscovered a relationship with God. It came with high reviews, and I was doing everything I could to avoid writing this chapter, so it seemed like the perfect escape for me. I curled up in my oversized leather chair, threw the down blanket over my lap, placed my bowl of popcorn on the table, and settled in for what I assumed would be a feel-good—happily ever after— movie.

This movie TORE MY HEART OUT. I was completely mistaken about the storyline. Instead of a movie about a man committing adultery, embezzling from his company, and hitting rock bottom, this movie was about a man who lost his daughter. I won't go into the details just in case you ever want to see the movie yourself, but for me, this movie transported me back to a time in my life that I thought had been packaged in a simple little box with a pretty pink bow. One of those moments I had checked off as finished, complete, and healed. I could not have been more wrong.

It was 1986. Thirty-two years ago, this month, actually. My ex-husband and I had just moved to El Paso Texas. He was in the military, so our life meant moving every few years from duty station to duty station. We had just returned home from our tour of Germany. I was twenty-two years old with two beautiful little girls ages three-and-a-half and fifteen months. Upon arrival at Fort Bliss, we stayed in guest housing for a few days while searching for a place to live. Our names were placed on the Base Housing waiting list, so we searched in the nearby community. The change of climates was a difficult transition. Texas in June is not always a fun place to be if you aren't used to high humidity, but we found a cute two-bedroom apartment right outside the base and moved in—just as the stomach flu seemed to hit.

Both my husband and older daughter were struck first. Two days later, the baby seemed to follow. We had just moved into our apartment, we had no phone hook-up yet, no car, and we didn't know anybody. After about two days of the stomach flu, Melissa, our fifteen-month-old, didn't seem to be getting better. She was running a fever and couldn't keep anything down. I was starting to get worried and decided the next day that I would figure out a way to take a taxi and get her to the local military hospital if there was no improvement. Just like every other normal night, I put her to bed in her crib, gave her Tylenol for her fever, and went to bed. It would not be long before I found out that this night was anything but normal.

The next morning, I heard a sound from her bedroom. It was almost like a happy yell, the kind she would let out when she was up and ready to play. I smiled in my bed, thinking she must be feeling better, thankful to have her well again. I took my time getting dressed before I made my way over to her room. When I opened the door, I could see her lying in her crib, on her back, just staring at the ceiling. I spoke to her, but she didn't respond. There was white foam around her mouth. She was cool and clammy to the touch.

I picked her up. She was limp in my arms. I started to scream. I put her back in the crib and ran out of my apartment. We had no phone. I didn't know what to do. I ran up and down the hall of that apartment building, banging on doors, screaming for someone to help me, to call an ambulance, to do something. Thankfully, someone opened the door and called for help. I wrapped Melissa up in a blanket and ran to the parking lot to meet the ambulance. When they arrived, the paramedic grabbed her out of my arms and started working on her. She was unresponsive to their attempts.

We arrived at the hospital a few minutes later, and the staff immediately whisked Melissa into a room and started working on her. My husband arrived. I don't even know how he knew, but the military is great about things like that. I was not allowed to stay in the room with her, as she was surrounded by doctors and nurses. Every few moments they would come out and ask us questions about her health. They tested her for aids, meningitis, and multiple other diseases that would manifest with similar symptoms. Everything was negative. They moved her up to ICU— still unresponsive—connected to tubes and machines that left her unrecognizable. The medical prognosis was not good. The doctors explained that sometime the night before, the fever Melissa had been struggling with, had most likely spiked to a fatal high. This high fever caused her little body to go into convulsions, and then septic shock, which left her without oxygen for an unspecified period of time. This is what they surmised caused her current condition of unresponsiveness. She was intubated and was breathing with the help of a machine.

For the next ten days, doctors and nurses surrounded her bedside. Due to the lack of oxygen in her system, my baby's internal organs started to fail one by one. First, she went into cardiac arrest, and they resuscitated her. Next, her liver failed. Her kidneys followed soon after. She started retaining water, and her tiny body was unrecognizable. Then one morning, on the tenth day, the doctors told me that she had no brain activity. My sweet little girl, they told me, was brain-dead.

Looking back, I have very little memory of the actual events. I remember her organs failing; I remember the doctors telling me she would likely not recover from this, and that we needed to prepare ourselves. I remember asking so many questions that I probably drove the nurses and doctors crazy. I remember praying in the hospital chapel for her to be healed, for this nightmare to be over, for God to allow me to take her home. I remember sitting next to her crib longing to hear the word "Mama" and see her beautiful little smile again. I don't remember where my husband was or my other daughter, I have no memory of that. I also have no memory of breaking down and crying. I never believed she would not come home with us. I was convinced she would wake up at any moment, so I would not allow pain to set in.

It was time to disconnect the tubes keeping her alive. I was still convinced the doctors did not know what they were talking about. My baby would wake up…we were going home. I sat in a white wooden rocking chair next to her crib as they removed the tubes. The nurse placed her gently in my arms. It was the first time I had held my baby in the last ten days. I rocked her back and forth, smiling down at her as I waited for her to open her eyes. My husband stood behind the chair. There was a priest behind him praying last rites—I hated him! I wanted him to go away. The more he prayed, the harder I rocked in that chair. The nurse told me that my husband should have a turn to rock her. I screamed no and held Melissa closer. Why wasn't she waking up? Why wasn't she opening her eyes? I rubbed her little cheeks, swollen from the water retention. I held her little hand and could feel her heartbeat pulsing through her skin. I continued to rock her as her pulse slowed down. I was numb; her pulse became slower and slower. And slower. Then…nothing. Very calmly, I told the nurse I was no longer feeling a pulse. She placed her stethoscope over Melissa's heart and confirmed what I already knew. My baby was gone.

I don't know what happened next. I have no clear recollection. I'm sure I rocked her more. I'm sure my husband held her — at least I hope he did. The next thing I remember is lying her back in her hospital crib and pulling the blankets up to cover her — just like they did in the movies. Then I left.

The funeral was the hardest thing I have ever had to deal with. I remember very little of the details. My husband and I went to the funeral home to view her body. I placed her favorite stuffed clown in her coffin. I was unemotional. The body I looked at was not my daughter. It was like living in a dream that turned into a nightmare. It was a cruel joke; it was not real, I would not allow 'them' to break me. During the church service, they wheeled the coffin to the front of the church, and the priest prayed. "She's in a better place," he said. I shook from the tears, trying desperately to hold it together. How could she be in a better place? Her place was with me, her mother. Nothing made sense.

At the gravesite — my only clear memory — I wanted everyone to leave. I struggled desperately with the thought of placing my baby in the dark, cold ground. It seemed barbaric, cruel, and inhuman. The guilt I felt was paralyzing. Everyone was watching me. I wanted to run. I wanted to pick up my baby and run away. I wanted to be left alone. I felt helpless as I worked so hard to keep in control, not wanting anyone to see me fall apart, yet drowning inside from a sorrow that I had never felt before.

I longed for the times I was alone. This was when I could let all my emotions come to the surface. I would sob loudly— screaming out, "Why"—my body shaking from the tremors of my grief. I wish I could say that I turned to God at this time and that he gave me peace, but I was so angry at God, hating Him for taking away my baby. So angry that He didn't save her, and feeling completely betrayed by the faith I had placed all my hopes in. These times of being alone were the only times I allowed myself to fall apart. In front of my husband or my daughter, or friends, however, I remained sad but collected— never allowing them to see what was going on inside. I never realized that then…I only realize that today.

As I thought more about my daughters comment tonight. Oh, you're THAT person, and when I thought about losing Melissa, I began to realize that this is what she was talking about. She was referring to the person who holds everything in, the person who thinks they're "over it." The person who is afraid to be vulnerable, who always has to look like she has it all together. THAT PERSON. The one who fears judgment, the one who is ashamed of her own feelings, the person who is embarrassed to break down for fear of ridicule, blame, or any other form of condemnation that someone might have. Even worse, the judgment she holds on herself.

It has been this way for as long as I can remember. As a child growing up in an abusive alcoholic home, there is not a day that I can remember not being beaten, hit, or dragged by my hair across a room by my mother. I was the first live birth after two miscarriages, but I don't think my mother ever loved or wanted me. I was a constant disappointment. I was bold, I was argumentative, and I had a strong will that she always wanted to break. Every day was a battle. Her weapons of choice could be a wooden board that we called the ABC stick because it had letters on it, a leather cat-o-nine tail (a type of whip with leather tails), the tall wooden fork or spoon that hung on our kitchen wall, or simply her hands. Hair pulling was her favorite—and it was constant. Regardless of the behavior I was being punished for, I believe the most infuriating thing for her was the fact that I would not react to her beatings. From as far back as I can remember, I would never cry during any of it. I would allow her to pull my hair across the room, I would deal with the ABC stick and the cat-o-nine tail, and I would simply glare back at her. When she would scream, "Do you want me to hit you again?" I would remain stone-face—not caring one way or another. It was my way of not being vulnerable, of not allowing her to get to me. I realize now that this behavior was simply a protective mechanism I learned very early on in life, a way to deal with and get through the pain. I would disconnect, leave my body almost, not feel anything, and certainly never allow myself to break.

Isn't it amazing how the mind works? In the darkest moments of my life, an escape route was created. A cave where I could retreat, where I couldn't feel, where I was protected from all of it. My very own safe-haven in the eye of the storm. It has served me well over the years, but I am realizing now that I no longer need to hide.

I've heard it said that feelings buried alive never truly die. They are always there, clawing their way to the surface, showing up in different circumstances of our lives, disguised as behaviors and reactions that are almost automatic—done subconsciously without our even knowing they are there. Sometimes they manifest themselves as shame. Shame of who we are, what we do, what we feel. Sometimes they manifest themselves as fear. Fear of stepping outside our comfort zones, fear of dreaming big, fear of getting too close to people, fear of letting people in. Sometimes they manifest themselves as detachment or disinterest. We become aloof to the things around us; not open to feeling pain or even joy. We simply exist, holding a part of us back; participating safely in this thing called life. Much like wondering how after thirty plus years, a simple plot to a movie can take me back as if it was yesterday and leave me crying in a helpless heap on the floor.

Being open to my own vulnerabilities in this book has been a liberating step for me. Linking arm and arm with my sister co-authors in sharing such a private, such a sacred piece of myself that I have never been willing to share before in the hope that others will no longer choose to suffer alone has been empowering. It has meant admitting to the world and even myself that I am human. I do not always have it all together. I am not perfect, nor do I have to be. I can let my guard down and allow others to help me shoulder the pain. Isn't that what life is about? Isn't that what this entire book and movement are meant to be about? Women supporting one another, women sharing their pain so that others can see that they aren't alone, women reaching out to their sisters and offering to lift them, to help them rise into the person they were created to be—without judgment, without jealousy, without competition.

This is OUR story.

This is OUR mission.

This is OUR movement.

It is OUR time!

Susan Ackerman

Susan has always known she would play a role in empowering women to step into their greatness. After watching so many women succumb to their own limited beliefs; not believing they were good enough, smart enough, young, enough, old enough— and having fought those same limited beliefs her entire life, she knew that something needed to be done. She believed that if women could work together, support each other, and raise each other up—in a positive and inspirational environment—that amazing things could happen.

Susan Ackerman is the founder and director of Inspire Reno and the visionary behind the Reno Rising project. It is her dream to create a global movement of women lifting women—without competition, without jealousy, and without judgment. The book you hold in your hands, *Reno Rising* is the first volume in her *Rising Across America* series.

Susan is the mom to three daughters: Tanya, Nicole, and Heather. She is s certified women's empowerment coach, speaker and author. She is a personal development junkie, avid reader, and future world traveler. Susan invites you personally to become part of this journey!

From the Photographer's Eye

We all hunger to discover our hidden talent, gifts, and purpose. After twenty-four years in a career creating portraits for people all over the world, I have discovered these two powerful things we have in common: purpose and a hero's journey.

We love watching this on the big screen, when someone gets knocked down and gets back up to fight for the bigger picture in life, to matter and to make a difference! We all hunger for our purpose.

Watching women discover their voice, strength, and charisma has become a true love of mine. We want to meet life with a sense of intention, presence, and power. I see this no matter what part of the world I am in. I also see the dance we are faced to partake in with fear, self-doubt and the tape we play over and over in our heads of words that DO NOT serve us!

No matter how successful someone has been in their life—when that annoying tape of negative words starts it's up to US to stop the tape, hit eject, and move on to our TRUTH!

We can learn, grow, share, and move forward, for now is the time for action!

Reno Rising is just this, women rising to serve their purpose and to change the landscape of their community for the better!

Watching women rise, take action, and plow through any hesitance has been a true blessing to witness. Holding the camera and documenting their journey has given me a front-row seat to witness their amazing transformations.

Taylor Boone,
Photographer,
Reno Rising.

Conclusion

It was early February 2018. I was just completing an Inspire Reno tour with a couple that I now consider my friends. The wife had recently become a member and wanted to show her husband the historic home that was now our office. After discussing the architecture, the history of the building and my upcoming plans for Inspire Reno and its future, we landed on a discussion of women's empowerment. I shared with him my passion for creating a community of like-minded women, a place where women in the Reno community could be supported, encouraged, and challenged to step into their greatness; a place where women would then support, encourage and challenge others to step into theirs.

Our conversation continued. He was excited for the idea of such a place to exist. He shared that he, too, believed that women had the potential to do anything they wanted to do, be anyone they wanted to be, accomplish anything they wanted to accomplish. He believed women had the power to change the world—and here's the part that gives me goose-bumps—if we simply locked arms with one another and worked together.

Did you hear that, my friend? You and I have the POWER to change the world simply by locking arm and arm and working TOGETHER. Does this get you as excited as I am about it?

Never in our history has there been a more perfect time for women to rise—together—to make a difference in our communities, in our states, and in our world. We need to stand united, arm in arm, lifting each other up, supporting each other, and encouraging each other. It is time for women everywhere to work together and not against each other. We need to finally understand that alone we can accomplish some, but together we can move mountains.

This is the purpose of *Reno Rising*. The women who shared their stories in the book you just read want you to know that you are not alone. We all have stories; we all have challenges; we all have obstacles… The great news is that we all have choices. We can choose what we do going forward. We can choose to hide from our circumstances, or we can use them as a stepping stone to change our circumstances. Everything we do from this moment forward is a choice. What choice are you now going to make?

You have reached the end of our book, but please know that this is only the beginning. It is a call to action, my dear friends. We personally invite you to join us on our mission to make a positive difference in the world. Share this book with a woman you know. Start a book discussion group. Reach out to the co-authors of this book—let us support you. Do you have a story to tell? We invite you to inquire about participating in the next volume of our series.

You will find us and all available resources at
www.renorising.com

You have a choice!

This is your time!

You were created for greatness!

CPSIA information can be obtained
at www.ICGtesting.com
Printed in the USA
FSHW01n1302290818
51863FS